THE

BUILD YOUR BOWL
Salad Cookbook

THE BUILD YOUR BOWL Salad Cookbook

75 Recipes for Healthy Salad Bowls
to Support Everyday Wellness

NINA CHERIE FRANKLIN, PhD
"That Salad Lady"

Quarto.com

First Published in 2025 by Fair Winds Press,
an imprint of The Quarto Group, 100 Cummings Center, Suite 265-D,
Beverly, MA 01915, USA. T (978) 282-9590 F (978) 283-2742

Fair Winds Press titles are also available at discount for retail, wholesale, promotional, and bulk purchase. For details, contact the Special Sales Manager by email at specialsales@quarto.com or by mail at The Quarto Group, Attn: Special Sales Manager, 100 Cummings Center, Suite 265-D, Beverly, MA 01915, USA.

29 28 27 26 25 2 3 4 5

ISBN: 978-0-7603-9677-3

Digital edition published in 2025
eISBN: 978-0-7603-9678-0

Library of Congress Cataloging-in-Publication Data
Franklin, Nina Cherie, author.
The build your bowl salad cookbook : 75 recipes for healthy salad bowls to support everyday wellness / Nina Cherie Franklin, PhD, "That Salad Lady".
Beverly, MA, USA : Fair Winds, 2025. | Includes bibliographical references and index. | LCCN 2025004648 (print) | LCCN 2025004649 (ebook) | ISBN 9780760396773 (trade paperback) | ISBN 9780760396780 (ebook)
1. Salads. 2. Side dishes (Cooking) 3. Cookbooks.
LCC TX740 .F6588 2025 (print) | LCC TX740 (ebook) | DDC 641.83—dc23/eng/20250208
LC record available at https://lccn.loc.gov/2025004648
LC ebook record available at https://lccn.loc.gov/2025

Design and page layout: Laura Shaw Design
Cover Image: Michelle Miller Photography
Photography: Michelle Miller Photography, except pages 12, 24, 28, 32, 43, 44, 66, 86, 108, 128, and 150 are Nina Cherie Franklin, PhD

Printed in USA

To my husband, Woody, who saw my potential before I ever did. This journey wouldn't be possible without your unwavering belief in me. And to our boys, Ramsey and Little Aubrey, my daily sources of strength and inspiration, who remind me every day why I pour my heart into this work.

Contents

Introduction

"I'll just eat a salad." Most of us have said this at some point in our lives when trying to make a healthier choice. It's often the easiest option in today's fast-paced world where choosing healthy foods can seem overwhelming. Unfortunately, the wellness industry often adds to the confusion with conflicting advice, unfulfilled diet promises, and a constant stream of new food trends. One day we're told to avoid carbs. The next day, they're essential. One expert touts the benefits of a high-protein diet, while another warns against it. With so much noise, it's no wonder we often feel lost when trying to eat healthy.

Even something as simple as the salad can be part of this puzzle. Despite its reputation as a healthy choice, making a salad that we actually want to eat can be surprisingly tricky. Not all salads are nutritionally equal, either.

Still, we order them at restaurants, buy them premade, or, with good intentions, try to make them at home by adding whatever we think will taste good. How many times have you bought a big batch of fresh ingredients only to throw them out later? Apologies to all the spring mix greens that have gone to waste, the wilted and rotten tomatoes, and that bottle of dressing way past its expiration date.

But what if I told you that making salads at home can be just as satisfying and far less wasteful? Imagine having the know-how to build a delicious bowl in minutes using fresh ingredients that won't end up in the trash. Think of creating a salad that not only tastes amazing but also supplies a full day's worth of fruits, vegetables, and other whole foods, providing you with all the essential vitamins, minerals, and antioxidants your body needs.

That's exactly where this book comes in.

Before we dive into the layers of this book, let me introduce myself. I'm Nina, but you might know me as "That Salad Lady" from my blog and social media channels. I'm not just a lady who loves salads, though—I'm also a healthy living coach with a PhD in Kinesiology, Nutrition, and Rehabilitation. For over two decades, I've been helping clients make sustainable changes to their diets and overall health. My goal is to simplify healthy eating and make it accessible to everyone, no matter their circumstances.

Like many of you, I've faced my share of struggles. I've lived through poverty and homelessness, battled food addiction and obesity, and navigated personal challenges like multiple miscarriages, anxiety, and depression.

"That Salad Lady" emerged from my own journey and a desire to support others who feel that their circumstances are barriers to achieving their health goals. Believe me, I've been there.

I grew up in the Englewood community on Chicago's South Side. A food desert by all accounts, my family faced the challenges of living well below the poverty line. In our household, salads were a rarity, and when they did make an appearance, iceberg lettuce was the only leafy green in our bowl. It was cheap and easy to come by. The monotony of this particular lettuce didn't spark any joy in my meals, and being a picky eater, I wasn't open to exploring other raw vegetables either.

It wasn't until my college years, immersed in health and nutrition studies, that I started to reimagine and ultimately embrace salads. I began to venture out of the typical garden blends and into a world of vibrant, nutrient-dense options like sweet bell peppers, roasted beets, and the oh-so-savory and creamy avocado. I experimented with a vegan diet and intermittent fasting (I still follow the latter), and I discovered the magic of combining flavors and textures to build complete and satisfying bowls.

Years later, I created "That Salad Lady" to inspire others to embrace the simplicity, versatility, and benefits of salad-based meals. As a scientist, I fully immersed myself in experimenting with different ingredients. My kitchen became my lab where I tested flavors, textures, and nutritional balances. In doing so, I discovered that building a great salad is both an art *and* a science.

It wasn't just about making a meal. It was about transforming how I approached food, health, and wellness. This realization led to the development of my "Build Your Bowl" system, a comprehensive yet simple guide that makes healthy eating more approachable, sustainable, and enjoyable.

Rather than solely counting calories, following restrictive diets, or obsessing over macronutrients, the Build Your Bowl system focuses on building balanced bowls by prioritizing nutrient-dense foods and mindful eating practices.

In this book, you'll discover every detail of the system and get a chance to apply it in every recipe. Each of the recipes in this book is vibrant, flavorful, and nutritious, crafted to save you time, reduce food waste, and boost your confidence in making healthy choices.

All ingredients are categorized into clear-cut whole food groups with nutritional analyses included to help you understand the hows and whys of building your bowls layer by layer to achieve lifelong wellness.

It doesn't stop at recipes, either. I also offer practical tips on meal prep, smart shopping, and selecting the right kitchen tools, all aimed at making healthy eating an effortless process.

The simple strategies I'm sharing here have really helped my clients and can truly make a difference in how you eat. Whether you're a busy parent juggling multiple responsibilities, a health-conscious individual ready to escape diet fads, a newcomer learning to make informed food choices, someone on a budget seeking healthy eating solutions, or a die-hard foodie who just loves a good salad, this book has something for you.

My goal here is for you to see that every bowl is an opportunity to nourish your body and mind, while exploring new flavors and textures. Each bowl you create can help you build healthier habits and a deeper understanding of what your body needs to thrive. By joining me on this journey, you'll rebuild your relationship with food, boost your eating confidence, and achieve lifelong wellness one bowl at a time.

So, let's build your bowl and your life.

—Nina Cherie Franklin, *aka* "That Salad Lady"

Getting the Most Out of This Book

This book is your guide to making salads that are both delicious and deeply nourishing, using straightforward methods you can easily follow. It's all about simplifying healthy eating and empowering you to build balanced, satisfying meals with ease.

To get the most out of this book, I encourage you to read through everything. Each chapter builds on the next, and the more you explore, the more confident you'll feel in creating bowls that work for you. Here's how you can make the most of it:

1. START WITH THE BUILD YOUR BOWL SYSTEM

Before you jump into the recipes, take a little time to get familiar with my Build Your Bowl system in chapter 1: The Basics of Building Your Bowl. This system is the foundation of the book, and it'll show you how to layer key ingredients—non-starchy veggies, fruits, high-quality proteins, whole food fats, and fiber-rich starches—into balanced bowls that fit your lifestyle. Whether you follow the recipes exactly or create your own combinations, the Build Your Bowl system gives you the flexibility to build meals that are healthy, satisfying, and full of flavor.

2. EXPLORE THE RECIPES, BUT KEEP AN OPEN MIND

I've grouped the recipes into themed chapters to make it simple to find what you're looking for:

CHAPTER 3: Effortless No-Cook & Easy Prep Bowls
CHAPTER 4: Power-Packed High-Protein Bowls
CHAPTER 5: Vibrant Vegan & Vegetarian Bowls
CHAPTER 6: Satisfying Low-Carb & Keto Bowls
CHAPTER 7: Nourishing Heart-Healthy Bowls
CHAPTER 8: Revitalizing Detox & Anti-Inflammatory Bowls

That said, don't feel limited by these categories. Many recipes fit into more than one theme. Think of the chapters as a starting point, but feel free to get creative and try new combinations. Mix and match ingredients and adapt recipes to your tastes and nutritional goals. For tips on substitutions and ingredient swaps, check out the "Common Ingredient Swaps for Meal Prep" table in chapter 2: Going Beyond the Bowl. It'll help you easily customize meals to fit your needs.

3. UNDERSTAND THE RECIPE LAYOUTS

Every recipe in this book is crafted with clarity and convenience in mind. Each one includes:

- Ingredients lists and step-by-step instructions that are easy to follow, no matter your skill level in the kitchen.

- Nutritional analyses that provide breakdowns of calories, fat, carbohydrates, protein, and other key details per serving.
- Build Your Bowl system profiles, showing how the recipe fits within the framework, highlighting elements like non-starchy veggies, whole food fats, high-quality proteins, and more.
- Customization ideas that allow you to tweak the recipe to your liking or dietary needs.

4. TAKE ADVANTAGE OF MEAL PREP TIPS

In chapter 1, I've included tips on meal prepping, smart shopping, and organizing your kitchen. These strategies will help you save time, reduce food waste, and ensure you always have what you need on hand to build your bowls. Planning ahead makes healthy eating effortless, so you find it easier to stay on track with your healthy habits.

5. FOCUS ON WHOLE FOOD NUTRITION

One of the core principles of this book is a focus on whole, nutrient-dense foods, which is emphasized in chapters 1 and 2. Each recipe is designed to give you the essential vitamins, minerals, and antioxidants your body needs to feel its best. When you focus on whole foods, you'll not only nourish your body, but you'll also notice how much better you feel inside and out.

6. PRACTICE MINDFUL EATING

One of the most important things I want you to take away from this book is the idea of mindful eating. Chapter 2: Going Beyond the Bowl goes into detail about how it can transform your relationship with food. It's not just about what you eat, but how you eat. Take time to enjoy the flavors, textures, and aromas of each bowl you create. By slowing down and really savoring your food, you'll connect more deeply with what you're eating, which makes healthy choices feel more natural.

7. READ IT ALL FOR THE FULL EXPERIENCE

I truly encourage you to read through each chapter. Every section offers something valuable, from meal prep tips and kitchen tools, to flavor combinations and mindful eating practices. This book is more than just a collection of recipes. It's your roadmap to building a healthier, more empowered relationship with food, one bowl at a time. By reading everything, you'll be better equipped to build bowls that are both delicious and aligned with your personal health goals. You'll walk away with the knowledge and confidence to make healthy eating a lifestyle, not just a temporary habit.

So, dig in and enjoy the journey! Start with the basics, try out some recipes, and make it your own. You've got this!

1 The Basics of Building Your Bowl

Contrary to popular belief, a salad isn't just a bowl of "rabbit food." It doesn't have to be a meal of abstention either. It can be a satisfying, nutrient-packed dish that leaves you feeling full and energized. In this chapter, I'll share some essential bowl-building basics, including an official introduction to my Build Your Bowl system. But before you can embrace the basics, you have to start reimagining salad making.

Now, you might be thinking, "Making a salad isn't difficult." And really, it isn't. Throw together some lettuce, cucumber, and tomato, squeeze out your favorite bottled dressing, maybe top it off with chicken or salmon, and you've made a salad. But why do we often limit ourselves to these basic, often bland, combinations?

Personally, I think it's because we've been conditioned to view salads as something we *should* eat rather than something we want to eat. We use them as a way to avoid foods we think we *shouldn't* have.

It's time to break free from this mindset and start thinking outside the bowl. The secret to transforming salads from bland to brilliant is rethinking our perceptions of different foods and their combinations. It's about dismissing some of the "rules" that may have been instilled in our heads about what, when, and how we should be eating.

Most important, it's about embracing salad making as the art form it truly is.

The Art of Layering for the Perfect Bowl

With the Build Your Bowl system at the forefront, this book offers a path to creating endless healthy salads. While each chapter is packed with delicious recipes, you don't actually *need* to follow a single one. As long as you understand how to use the system, you can easily build your own wholesome bowls tailored to your tastes and preferences. When it comes to salad making, the possibilities are endless. It's all about how you choose, use, and most important, enjoy your layers.

In the Build Your Bowl system, "layers" are simply the ingredients you build your bowl with. Each layer adds its own unique texture, flavor, and nutritional benefit, and together they form a beautiful masterpiece of satisfaction and nourishment. Layering might seem like a bit of an art at first because it is. But it's an art you can master. With a little practice, you'll quickly gain the skill and confidence to build bowls effortlessly, whether you're following a recipe or not.

The basics of building your bowl revolve around combining layers in ways that align with your food preferences, lifestyle, and wellness goals. I always say that layering is an opportunity for experimentation, self-expression, and creativity. Rather than thinking about the actual ingredients themselves, first think about the eating experience you're trying to create.

Instead of focusing on all the foods you think you "can't" or "shouldn't" eat, focus on what you can and actually *want* to eat. What types of foods do you normally like? Are there certain food colors you find more visually appealing than others? Do you prefer simple or extravagant salads?

Whether you're aiming for a nutrient-packed meal, a light and refreshing snack, or a hearty and satisfying dinner, the Build Your Bowl system helps you achieve it. Soon, you'll be creating delicious and vibrant salads, and finding it much easier to get in the daily nutrients your body needs.

Mastering the Build Your Bowl System

Build Your Bowl emphasizes whole food nutrition as the cornerstone for creating balanced and satisfying meals. It's an ingredient-based approach to mindful eating, which we'll discuss more in chapter 2. The idea is simple. Every whole food ingredient is unique and brings something special to both your body and your bowl. The system includes five core whole food groups that you're probably familiar with:

1. Non-Starchy Vegetables
2. Assorted Fruit Varieties
3. Whole Food Fat Sources
4. High-Quality Proteins
5. Fiber-Rich Starches

Depending on your eating preferences, you might not include all of these food groups in every meal and that's perfectly fine. The key is knowing how to strategically combine them to suit your unique wellness goals and then eat them in suitable portions to reap their benefits.

We'll talk about specific strategies for incorporating these whole food groups into your daily meals in later sections. But for now, let's focus on understanding the unique qualities of each food group and how they contribute to a well-rounded diet.

TABLE 1: THE BUILD YOUR BOWL SYSTEM		
Food Group	**Examples**	**Benefits**
Non-Starchy Vegetables **(6–8 servings/day)**	Leafy greens (lettuces including romaine, endive, watercress, butter and leaf; spinach, arugula, chard, dandelion leaves, Swiss chard, beet greens)	Tender and nutrient dense, provide antioxidants, rich in vitamin K for bone health and blood clotting
	Cruciferous vegetables (kale, broccoli, cauliflower, Brussels sprouts, cabbage, bok choy, collard greens, mustard greens, turnip greens, radishes, turnips)	Hearty and high in fiber, contain cancer-fighting compounds
	Colorful choices (bell peppers, tomatoes, carrots, beets, red onions, chile peppers, red cabbage, radicchio, eggplant)	Vibrant and sweet, packed with antioxidants, enhance immune function and skin health
	Fresh and crisp (cucumbers, zucchini, celery, snap peas, jicama, green beans, kohlrabi, fennel)	Cool and crunchy, high in water content, support hydration and digestion
	Unique flavors (asparagus, mushrooms, leeks, artichokes, okra, scallions, garlic, shallots, parsnips)	Distinctive and savory, provide a variety of flavors, rich in gut-friendly fibers
Assorted Fruit Varieties **(2–4 servings/day)**	Berries (blueberries, strawberries, raspberries, blackberries, pomegranate, cranberries, elderberries, mulberries, grapes)	Sweet and tangy flavors, high in fiber and antioxidants, support immune health and improve digestion
	Citrus fruits (oranges, grapefruits, tangerines, lemons, limes, clementines, mandarins, pomelos, kumquats)	Refreshing and zesty, rich in vitamin C, enhance immune function and aid digestion
	Tropical fruits (pineapple, mango, papaya, kiwi, guava, passion fruit, lychee, jackfruit, starfruit, dragon fruit)	Sweet and exotic, packed with antioxidants, support immune health and improve digestion
	Stone fruits (peaches, plums, cherries, apricots, nectarines)	Juicy and sweet, provide antioxidants, promote skin health
	Dried fruits (cranberries, raisins, dates, figs, apricots, prunes, goji berries, currants, blueberries, cherries)	Sweet and chewy; high in antioxidants, boost energy levels
Whole Food Fat Sources **(3–5 servings/day)**	Fatty fruits (avocado, olives, coconut, durian, açaí berries)	Rich and savory flavors, provide monounsaturated fats, support heart health and satiety
	Nuts (almonds, walnuts, cashews, pecans, pistachios, Brazil nuts, macadamia nuts, hazelnuts, pine nuts, chestnuts)	Crunchy and nutrient dense, high in fiber and antioxidants, support brain health and reduce inflammation
	Seeds (chia seeds, flaxseed, pumpkin seeds/pepitas, sunflower seeds, hemp seeds, sesame seeds, poppy seeds)	Tiny and powerful, packed with omega-3 fatty acids and fiber, support digestive health and reduce inflammation

TABLE 1: THE BUILD YOUR BOWL SYSTEM		
Food Group	**Examples**	**Benefits**
Whole Food Fat Sources (cont.) **(3–5 servings/day)**	Protein-packed fats (natural cheeses, yogurt, egg yolks, fatty fish including salmon, tuna, trout, sardines, mackerel, herring, and anchovies)	Versatile and nutrient rich, high in a variety of fats, provide antioxidants, support muscle and brain health
	Oils and spreads (extra-virgin olive oil, avocado oil, coconut oil, flaxseed oil, hemp oil, sesame oil, walnut oil, macadamia nut oil, grapeseed oil, tahini, nut butters, seed butters)	Smooth and flavorful, high in antioxidants, support overall well-being
High-Quality Proteins **(3– 5 servings/day)**	Poultry (chicken, turkey, duck; ideally skinless and white meat)	Versatile and lean, rich in selenium for immune function, support muscle growth and repair
	Red meat (beef, pork, lamb; ideally lean cuts like sirloin or tenderloin)	Rich and hearty, high in iron and B vitamins, support muscle health and energy production
	Fish and seafood (salmon, tuna, trout, crab, shrimp, cod, haddock, sardines, mackerel, herring, clams)	Light and nutritious, high in omega-3s and other fatty acids, provide antioxidants, support muscle and brain health
	Dairy and eggs (natural cheeses and yogurt; ideally aged cheeses, Greek yogurt, kefir, egg whites, egg yolks)	Creamy and nutrient dense, high in calcium and probiotics, support bone and gut health
	Plant-based proteins (whole soy foods including tofu, tempeh, and edamame; chia seeds, hemp seeds, quinoa, amaranth, teff, buckwheat, kamut)	Diverse and filling, high in fiber and essential amino acids, support muscle growth and overall wellness
Fiber-Rich Starches **(1–4 servings/day)**	Whole grains (whole wheat, brown rice, farro, oats, barley, bulgur, wild rice, buckwheat, rye)	Hearty and filling, rich in magnesium for muscle and nerve function, provide sustained energy
	Starchy vegetables (sweet potatoes, purple potatoes, yams, corn, peas, taro, winter squash including pumpkin, acorn squash, and butternut squash)	Versatile and satisfying, rich in antioxidants, help regulate blood sugar levels and provide steady energy
	Legumes (lentils, chickpeas, black beans, kidney beans, black-eyed peas, navy beans, pinto beans, lima beans, mung beans, cannellini beans)	Savory and nutrient dense, packed with plant-based protein and iron, support heart health and muscle growth
	Ancient grains (quinoa, millet, teff, amaranth, spelt, sorghum, einkorn, kamut, fonio)	Nutty and wholesome, high in essential amino acids, support overall wellness
	Unique flavors (plantains, yucca, parsnips, sunchokes, Jerusalem artichokes, rutabagas, kohlrabi, celeriac, jicama)	Flavorful with diverse textures, rich in potassium for heart health and muscle function

NON-STARCHY VEGETABLES

You'll always get the most nutritional bang for your bowl by filling at least half of it with non-starchy vegetables. Aim for 2 to 4 one-cup servings of raw vegetables (1 to 2 cups cooked; weight varies, cooked or uncooked) per bowl, with a daily target of 6 to 8 servings in total. You can always eat more if you'd like!

Besides forming the bulk of your bowl, these veggies are the workhorses of a healthy diet. The deeper the colors, the richer they are in nutrients, especially phytonutrients. Phytonutrients are specialized plant-based compounds with antioxidant properties that protect against various chronic diseases and promote overall good health.

If you regularly count calories or carbs, or even if you're just watching your weight, you'll appreciate that non-starchy veggies are generally low in calories, and (with the exception of a few) very low in sugar. They're also high in dietary fiber, which comes with benefits ranging from weight loss to improved gut health. What's really nice about these veggies is that each brings its own unique taste and texture, enhancing the overall experience of your bowl.

Here are some non-starchy vegetables you can use to start building your bowl:

- **Leafy Greens:** Spinach, lettuces, arugula, chard, and dandelion leaves
- **Cruciferous Vegetables:** Kale, broccoli, cauliflower, Brussels sprouts, and cabbage
- **Colorful Choices:** Bell peppers, tomatoes, radishes, carrots, and beets
- **Fresh and Crisp:** Cucumbers, zucchini, celery, snap peas, and jicama
- **Unique Flavors:** Asparagus, green beans, mushrooms, leeks, and fennel

THE POWER OF PHYTONUTRIENTS

There are over 25,000 phytonutrients found in plants and the best way to get a good mix is by eating a variety of colorful veggies. Each color has its own unique set of phytonutrients and brings its own set of benefits.

On the red end of the spectrum, veggies like tomatoes and red bell peppers are packed with lycopene and beta-carotene, which have been shown to reduce the risk of certain cancers and improve heart health.

On the green side, vegetables like spinach and kale are rich in chlorophyll and lutein. These phytonutrients help detoxify the body and promote eye health. Eating a rainbow of these veggie layers can truly make you feel just as vibrant as they look.

So, when you're building your bowl, try to include at least three different colors. Think orange carrots, green spinach, and red bell peppers to get the most out of your phytonutrient intake.

ASSORTED FRUIT VARIETIES

Fruit is indeed nature's candy and a quick, easy, healthy way to upgrade your salad bowl. Include ½ to 1 cup of fresh fruit (weight varies) in each bowl, aiming for a total of 2 to 4 servings per day. Contrary to long-held food pairing myths, it's perfectly fine to eat fruits and vegetables together as you would in a salad. The deliciously sweet and tangy flavors of different fruits even help balance the bitterness of certain veggies, making them more pleasing to the palate. Even small amounts pack hefty doses of gut-friendly fiber and immune-boosting antioxidants. As with non-starchy veggies, deeply colored fruits house the most nutrients.

When it comes to dried fruits, they too can offer good nutrition. In fact, many dried fruits are even richer in antioxidants than their fresh counterparts. Just be mindful of their higher sugar content—a little goes a very long way. Stick to 1 to 2 tablespoons (weight varies) per bowl to enjoy their benefits without overdoing it. Whether fresh or dried, incorporating a variety of fruits into your salads not only enhances their nutritional value but also makes your meals more vibrant and enjoyable.

Here are some sweet, tangy, and refreshing fruits to add to your bowl:

- **Berries:** Blueberries, strawberries, raspberries, blackberries, and pomegranate
- **Citrus Fruits:** Oranges, grapefruits, tangerines, lemons, and limes
- **Tropical Fruits:** Pineapple, mango, papaya, kiwi, and guava
- **Stone Fruits:** Peaches, plums, cherries, apricots, and nectarines
- **Dried Fruits:** Cranberries, raisins, dates, figs, and apricots

Note that a handful of fruits, such as avocados and olives, are better classified as fats due to their relatively high fat content (see "Whole Food Fat Sources," following).

WHOLE FOOD FAT SOURCES

Though long treated as a dietary boogeyman, fat is actually a *must-have* layer in the Build Your Bowl system. That said, you don't want to overdo it. Include 1 to 2 servings of high-quality fat in each bowl, aiming for a daily total of 3 to 5 servings. For reference, one serving is equivalent to 1 tablespoon of oils (15 ml) or nut butters (16 g), one-quarter of an avocado, 2 tablespoons (weight varies) of nuts or seeds, 1 ounce (28 g) of cheese, 1 egg, or 3 ounces (84 g) of fatty fish.

Besides bringing loads of flavor to the bowl, fats help our bodies better absorb many of the vitamins and antioxidants housed in the veggie and fruit layers. This is why I often say that excluding fat defeats the purpose of eating a salad in the first place. Plus, fats keep you feeling full longer by slowing digestion and reducing the temptation to snack between meals.

Of the various types of fats, some are essential, meaning our bodies can't produce them on their own and must obtain them through our diet. These include omega-3 and omega-6 fatty acids, which are often called "good fats" due to their roles in promoting heart and brain health, supporting cell function, and maintaining healthy skin. Including even moderate amounts of these fats in your bowl is a sure way to savor their flavors while reaping health benefits.

Here are some nutrient-rich, flavorful fat sources you can use to start building your bowl:

- **Fatty Fruits:** Avocado, olives, coconut, durian, and açaí berries
- **Nuts:** Almonds, walnuts, cashews, pecans, and pistachios
- **Seeds:** Chia seeds, flaxseed, pumpkin seeds/pepitas, sunflower seeds, and hemp seeds
- **Protein-Packed Fats:** Natural cheeses, yogurt, egg yolks, and fatty fish (salmon, tuna, or trout)

THE FAT DILEMMA

Does the notion of "good" and "bad" fats confuse you? You're not alone! Much of this confusion comes from blanket generalizations about dietary fat.

Simply put, monounsaturated fats (found in avocados, nuts, and olive oil) and polyunsaturated fats (found in oily fish, seeds, and walnuts) are generally considered "good," while trans fats (found in processed foods) and some saturated fats (found in butter, coconut oil, and red meat) are labeled "bad."

When eaten in excess, trans fats, particularly the artificial ones found in many processed foods, can negatively impact health. However, the role of saturated fats is more debatable, adding to the confusion. Foods like full-fat yogurt, cheese, and coconut oil contain saturated fats but also offer health benefits like boosting HDL (good) cholesterol and providing essential nutrients.

Rather than labeling fats as good or bad, I encourage you to instead focus on the overall quality and source of the fat. Consider where it's coming from and how it fits into your overall diet. Including a variety of fats from plant-based foods like nuts, seeds, avocados, and oils in moderation can help support heart health and overall well-being.

- **Oils and Spreads:** Extra-virgin olive oil, avocado oil, tahini, nut butters, and seed butters

As you can see, some proteins also double as whole food fat sources. This is a win-win because it gives you a balanced mix of essential nutrients, supporting your overall health and making your meals even more nutritious and satisfying (see "High-Quality Proteins," below).

HIGH-QUALITY PROTEINS

In the Build Your Bowl system, high-quality proteins provide the essential amino acids your body needs to thrive. Whether animal or plant-based, adding high-quality lean protein to your salad can transform it from a simple side dish into a full meal. Aim for 1 to 2 servings of protein in each bowl, with a daily target of 3 to 5 servings from a mix of animal and plant-based sources. For reference, one serving is equivalent to 3 to 4 ounces of cooked poultry, meat, or fish, 1 whole egg, ½ cup (weight varies) of cooked beans, peas, or lentils, or 1 cup (weight varies) of a dairy food like yogurt.

High-quality proteins provide all the vital amino acids our bodies need. As the building blocks of protein, amino acids are crucial for repairing tissues, producing enzymes and hormones, and supporting overall growth and development. There are twenty standard amino acids. Nine are essential, meaning our bodies can't produce them and *must* get them through our diet, just like fats.

Ideal choices are nutrient dense and beneficial, such as skinless poultry, fish, egg whites, low-fat dairy, and plant-based options like tofu, quinoa, and edamame. Higher-fat options, like bacon or full-fat cheese, can be included

HOW MUCH PROTEIN DO YOU NEED?

The question of how much protein you need is just as layered as a salad. A good rule of thumb is to aim for a daily intake of 0.36 gram of protein per pound (0.8 grams per kilogram) of body weight. So, if you weigh 150 pounds (or 68 kilograms), you'd need about 54 grams of protein daily. But if you're an athlete or highly active, you might need more—somewhere around 0.5 to 0.8 gram per pound (1.2 to 1.7 grams per kilogram) of body weight depending on your activity level.

occasionally as flavor enhancers rather than primary protein layers.

From a nutritional standpoint, animal-based proteins like meat, fish, and dairy foods are considered complete proteins because they contain all nine essential amino acids. Some plant-based proteins, such as whole soy foods, and certain seeds and grains, also fall into this category. However, a large majority of plant-based proteins, like beans, nuts, and most seeds and grains, are incomplete on their own. This is why pairing and mixing proteins is key, regardless of your eating style.

If your diet is entirely plant based, combining foods like beans and rice, chickpeas and farro, or lentils and whole-grain couscous ensures you get all the essential amino acids in your bowl. Incorporating complete protein sources like tofu, tempeh, and quinoa is particularly beneficial in ensuring a broad range of amino acids and nutrients.

Even for those who eat animal proteins, varying your sources helps maintain a balanced intake of nutrients and prevents overconsumption of any single type of protein.

Throughout this book, we'll explore creative ways to combine different proteins to build balanced bowls. For now, here are some examples of high-quality, complete proteins you can use to start building your bowl:

- **Poultry:** Chicken, turkey, and duck (ideally skinless and white meat)
- **Red Meat:** Beef, pork, and lamb (ideally lean cuts like sirloin or tenderloin)
- **Fish and Seafood:** Salmon, tuna, trout, crab, and shrimp
- **Dairy and Eggs:** Natural cheeses, whole eggs, and yogurt (ideally aged cheeses and Greek yogurt)
- **Plant-Based Proteins:** Whole soy foods (tofu, tempeh, edamame), chia seeds, hemp seeds, quinoa, and amaranth

FIBER-RICH STARCHES

You might be surprised that starches are included in the Build Your Bowl system since they're so often shunned. While refined starches like white bread, white rice, and pastries might not be ideal due to their lack of nutrients and effects on blood sugar, whole food fiber-rich starches like sweet potatoes, quinoa, and brown rice are excellent sources of health-promoting fiber and plant-based proteins.

This nutrient combination helps regulate blood sugar levels and provides steady energy, ensuring longer-lasting fullness and reducing the risk of crashes and cravings.

You can reap benefits by including as little as ¼ to ½ cup (weight varies) of fiber-rich starches

ANIMAL-BASED PROTEIN ALTERNATIVES

With the rise in veganism and plant-based diets, faux meat production has increased substantially. While these meat alternatives can be convenient, it's important to check labels for added sodium, preservatives, and other additives.

Despite being marketed as healthy, many of these products contain remarkably high levels of sodium and artificial ingredients that are not beneficial for long-term health. In other words, their risks outweigh their benefits.

When building your bowl, I encourage you to opt for whole food protein sources whenever possible. Foods like beans, lentils, nuts, seeds, and tofu not only offer protein but also bring loads of fiber and other nutrients to the bowl that processed alternatives often lack.

in each bowl, with a daily target of 1 to 4 servings, depending on your eating preferences or carbohydrate goals. For those following a low-carb diet, aim for the lower end of this range to stay within your carbohydrate targets.

If your diet is entirely plant-based, fiber-rich starches are especially great for rounding out your bowls. While most starches are incomplete proteins, strategically pairing them together, as with beans and rice, creates complete proteins.

Even if your diet *isn't* entirely plant based, adding such variety can bring other benefits too, such as boosting digestive health with fiber and improving nutrient absorption with healthy fats. Ultimately, these nutrient-dense options help you build satisfying and well-balanced meals.

Here are some hearty and versatile fiber-rich starches that will bring a variety of flavors and textures to your bowl:

- **Whole Grains:** Whole wheat, brown rice, farro, oats, and barley
- **Starchy Vegetables:** Sweet potatoes, corn, peas, taro, and winter squash (acorn or butternut)
- **Legumes:** Lentils, chickpeas, black beans, kidney beans, and black-eyed peas
- **Ancient Grains:** Quinoa, millet, teff, amaranth, and spelt
- **Unique Flavors:** Plantains, yucca, parsnips, sunchokes, and Jerusalem artichokes

You may have noticed that quinoa, buckwheat, kamut, teff, and amaranth also made the list of complete proteins. These grains are superstars in plant-based bowls as they help ensure you get all the essential nutrients your body needs.

THE FINISHING TOUCHES: FLAVOR ENHANCERS

Building your bowl with nutrient-dense layers is just the beginning. To make your salads really shine, you need those finishing touches that bring everything together. If you've ever felt like your salad was missing something, flavor enhancers are likely what it needs. Fresh herbs, spices, citrus, and savory elements like bacon and toasted nuts can transform your bowl from ordinary to amazing, adding depth, texture, and nutritional benefits.

TABLE 2: FLAVOR ENHANCERS FOR YOUR BOWL		
Type	**Examples**	**Benefits**
Herbs & Spices	Basil, mint, parsley, cilantro, dill, rosemary, thyme, oregano, chives, cumin, paprika, turmeric, garlic, ginger, red pepper flakes, black pepper, cinnamon	Add aromatic flavors, rich in antioxidants, anti-inflammatory properties
Citrus Juice & Zest	Lemon juice, lime juice, orange segments, grapefruit slices, lemon zest, lime zest, orange zest	Bring bright flavors, add tangy contrast, high in vitamin C
Oils & Vinegars	Extra-virgin olive oil, infused olive oils, toasted sesame oil, avocado oil, walnut oil, balsamic vinegar, apple cider vinegar, wine vinegars, rice vinegar, champagne vinegar	Enhance richness and depth, provide healthy fats, essential for nutrient absorption
Dairy Foods	Feta, goat cheese, mozzarella, parmesan, Gorgonzola, blue cheese, cheddar, Brie, ricotta, Swiss, cottage cheese, Greek yogurt, butter, ghee	Bring creaminess, savory flavor, good source of calcium
Crunchy & Savory Toppings	Roasted chickpeas, toasted walnuts, pumpkin seeds/pepitas, sunflower seeds, flaxseed, chia seeds, homemade croutons, crispy bacon bits, sliced almonds, pecans, cashews, pine nuts, sesame seeds	Add texture and flavor variety, contain essential nutrients, enhance satiety
Sweet Additions	Dried cranberries, raisins, apricots, dates, figs, dried cherries, mango strips, pineapple chunks, dried blueberries, dried strawberries, coconut flakes	Introduce natural sweetness and chewy texture, high in fiber, rich in antioxidants

Whether you're craving a burst of freshness, a hint of zest, or a touch of sweetness, the right combination of these elements can take your bowl to the next level. Many of these flavor enhancers, like citrus fruits, oils, and cheeses, also serve as foundational layers in the Build Your Bowl system. Table 2 (above) highlights a range of options along with their unique benefits. Use it as a guide to explore new combinations that suit your taste and nutritional goals.

No matter what you're making, these simple enhancements can make your bowl more enjoyable and satisfying. With these finishing touches, you'll find it easier to create delicious, visually appealing bowls that help you meet your daily nutrient needs.

THE SWEET TRUTH ABOUT SUGAR

I'd be remiss if I didn't address the topic of sugar because sugar is everywhere! While processed foods like candy, cookies, cakes, pastries, and soft drinks are obvious sources, it's the hidden sugars that really take a toll. These sugars are in unsuspecting foods, many of which are marketed as "healthy."

They're in bottled condiments, including salad dressings. They're flavor-enhancers for "low-fat" and "fat-free" foods. They're even in some plant-based milks and yogurts. Despite our best efforts, it's nearly impossible to eliminate sugar from our diets. And there's a good chance you're taking in a lot of it without even knowing it. So how do you cut down on sugar in such a sugar-laden world?

Following the Build Your Bowl system is one of the simplest solutions. The sugars found in the whole food groups are naturally occurring and come with dietary fiber, vitamins, and minerals that help moderate their effects on your blood sugar levels. Food pairings matter too. Combining sugars with fat and protein can slow absorption and prevent blood sugar spikes.

By focusing on whole fruits and vegetables, beans, and quality grains, you can enjoy the sweetness nature provides while also benefiting from the nutritional package that comes with it.

Indulging now and then is perfectly fine too. We're all human and deserve to occasionally enjoy life's little pleasures!

Shopping Tips for Building Brilliant Bowls

Now that you have a solid understanding of the core whole food groups in the Build Your Bowl system, you're ready to bring these layers into your kitchen with a well-planned trip to the grocery store.

With so many options in the aisles, it can sometimes feel overwhelming, even for the savviest shoppers! But remember, it's not about loading your cart with random produce. It's about ensuring your fridge and pantry are stocked with exactly what you need to build vibrant, nutrient-rich bowls that are both delicious and satisfying.

To get started, I've put together this list of essential tips to help you shop effortlessly and effectively, ensuring you always have the best ingredients on hand.

1. PLAN AHEAD

Before you even think about heading out to the grocery store, plan your meals for the week. This not only saves time but also helps you stay focused on buying only what you need, reducing unnecessary waste and expenses. Start by making a general list of the exact ingredients needed for your planned bowls, including a variety of non-starchy vegetables, fruits, whole food fat sources, high-quality proteins, and fiber-rich starches. Planning this way helps reduce impulse buys and ensures you have everything to create balanced bowls.

2. CHECK YOUR FRIDGE AND PANTRY

With your meal plan in hand, take stock of what you already have in your fridge and pantry. A quick inventory not only helps you

avoid duplicates and prevent food waste, but can also inspire meal ideas based on ingredients that need to be used up. This approach makes your shopping more cost-efficient, saves you time at the store, and keeps your kitchen organized.

3. CREATE A DETAILED SHOPPING LIST

After you've taken stock of what you already have, it's time to create a detailed shopping list. Write specific quantities to stay focused on your meal plan and avoid overbuying. I also suggest grouping items by grocery department. For instance, you might write:

- **Produce**: 1 head of romaine lettuce, 2 avocados, 3 bell peppers (1 red, 1 yellow, 1 green)
- **Dairy**: 1 block of feta cheese, 1 container of Greek yogurt
- **Proteins**: 1 pound of chicken breast, 1 package of tofu.

Trust me, this step will save you money and time while minimizing waste.

4. DECIDE WHEN TO GO ORGANIC

From an environmental sustainability standpoint, organic foods are undeniably great choices, but there's actually very little difference in the nutritional value between organic and conventional foods. So, when you're eyeing those organic options at the store, consider your budget first, as the markup can be as much as 80 percent! If you need to save money on your ingredients, there's no shame in choosing the best option for your budget. Ultimately, making informed choices that reflect your values and circumstances is what matters most.

5. BUY SEASONAL AND LOCAL PRODUCE

When it comes to grocery shopping, choosing seasonal fruits and vegetables is indeed a game changer! They're often fresher, tastier, and more affordable than out-of-season options. If you prefer organic produce, it's typically cheaper when in season too. Whether you opt for organic or conventional, local farmers' markets are excellent places to shop for seasonal produce. These markets not only offer high-quality ingredients but also support local agriculture. Plus, you'll know exactly where your produce comes from and often have the chance to learn about farming practices directly from the farmers.

6. FOCUS ON FRESHNESS

I can't stress enough how important it is to prioritize fresh produce for the best nutrition and flavor. Look for vibrant colors and firm textures. Tomatoes should be a deep red, bell peppers bright, and cucumbers firm. Steer clear of anything that looks dull, wilted, or brown spotted. Leafy greens like kale and spinach should have crisp, bright leaves. Fruits like avocados should be firm but not hard. And don't forget to give your produce a sniff. Fruits like melons, for instance, should have a pleasant aroma. Check stems and roots for freshness too. It takes a little practice, but you'll get better at it with time.

7. STOCK UP ON STAPLES

When it comes to bowl building, I highly recommend stocking up on pantry staples like beans, grains, nuts, seeds, and oils. Since these whole food layers have a relatively long shelf life, they can be bought in bulk, ensuring you always have essential ingredients for your bowls. Many of the recipes in this book call for layers like chickpeas, quinoa, chia seeds, flaxseed, and extra-virgin olive oil so you'll find yourself reaching for them a lot. They can also be used in a variety of recipes beyond your bowls. Think of them as the building blocks for many great meals, even when you're running low on fresh produce.

8. PAY ATTENTION TO FOOD LABELS

Checking the labels of packaged foods is a must, especially for dressings, oils, and canned goods like beans and peas. Start by looking at the serving size and servings per container to keep your portions in check. Remember, not all calories are equal, so be cautious with "low-calorie" or "fat-free" products since they often lack essential nutrients. Keep an eye out for additives like hydrogenated oils, excessive sodium, added sugars, artificial colors, and preservatives. These are signs the food is heavily processed. Finally, ensure the ingredients list is short and simple with recognizable whole foods.

Essential Kitchen Tools for Bowl Building

With your fridge and pantry stocked with salad ingredients for the layers, let's shift gears and talk about some essential bowl-building tools for your kitchen. Bowl building, as beneficial as it is, should be all about utility, efficiency, and convenience. It shouldn't be time-consuming, overwhelming, or stressful. The challenge often comes from not having the right tools to simplify the process.

As a healthy living coach, I've seen how the right tools take my clients' bowl-building skills to the next level. So, here I'm sharing the essential tools that'll make building the recipes in this book easier and transform your meal prep experience. In my opinion, these are *must-haves* for any kitchen!

1. CUTTING BOARDS

Cutting boards are a great investment. To prevent cross-contamination, I recommend having separate boards for meats and vegetables. Wooden boards are top choices for their durability and knife-friendly surface. Bamboo boards are also great and more sustainable too. Plastic and glass boards are economical and easy to clean but can dull your knives over time. Plus, glass boards might even chip. Choose wisely based on your needs and preferences.

2. SHARP KNIVES

A good set of knives is absolutely essential. Not just for bowl building, but for all sorts of meal prep. At the very least, invest in a quality chef's knife and a paring knife, along with a sharpener to maintain their edges. Sharp knives make chopping and slicing safer and more efficient. If you go for a set, consider self-sharpening knives, which come with a built-in sharpener in the storage block. So, every time you pull out or return a knife, it gets sharpened.

3. SALAD SPINNER

A salad spinner is one of those items you don't think you need until you actually have one. It's the most efficient tool for soaking, rinsing, and drying all types of salad greens, but its value doesn't stop there. You can also use it for herbs, mushrooms, berries, pastas, and even beans. Look for one with a sturdy base, large capacity, and an easy-to-use spinning mechanism. Once you start using it, you'll wonder how you ever managed without one!

4. MEASURING TOOLS AND MIXING BOWLS

You'll need a variety of cups, spoons, and bowls in different sizes for measuring, combining, and tossing your layers. These typically come in plastic, stainless steel, and glass varieties. Glass is perfect for wet ingredients as it doesn't absorb odors or stains and lets you see your ingredients clearly. Stainless steel is lightweight, durable, and easy to clean. Plastic is lighter and much cheaper but often retains flavors. It all boils down to your personal preference and general prepping needs.

5. GRATER, PEELER, PRESS, AND SQUEEZER

You can really elevate your bowl-building game with a good grater, peeler, garlic press, and citrus squeezer. A sturdy vegetable peeler with a comfortable grip and sharp blade quickly removes skins from certain veggies. A grater or microplane is perfect for adding zest, finely grated cheese, or shredded veggies. They're also great for grating garlic and ginger to enhance your dressings and marinades. A reliable garlic press makes adding freshly minced garlic easy, and with a citrus squeezer, you can effortlessly add fresh lemon or lime juice to your bowls.

6. CHOPPER AND SLICER

If you're not comfortable with knives, a vegetable chopper and mandoline slicer are invaluable tools for efficient bowl building. A good chopper can dice, chop, and slice various veggie layers like onions, peppers, and tomatoes quickly and consistently, saving you time and effort. Look for one with multiple blade attachments for versatility. Then there's the mandoline slicer, which is perfect for creating uniform, thin slices of veggies like cucumbers, radishes, and carrots. Choose one with adjustable thickness settings and a safety guard and be cautious when using it. Mandolines are extremely sharp. Always use the safety guard or wear protective gloves to prevent injury.

7. BLENDER OR FOOD PROCESSOR

When it comes to prepping salad layers, a good blender or food processor can save you a lot of time and effort. While a blender is perfect for creating smooth, creamy dressings, a food processor excels at chopping large quantities of vegetables, grinding nuts, and making chunky salsas. When choosing one, look for multiple speed settings, durable blades, and a large capacity for big batches. This book alone will show just how essential these appliances can be.

8. STORAGE CONTAINERS

Bowl building involves prepping a lot of layers, so keeping them fresh is crucial. That's why airtight containers are a must-have. You'll need various sizes to store layers like chopped veggies, cooked grains, and homemade dressings. Glass containers are great because they let you see your ingredients and don't retain odors. If you prefer plastic, make sure they're BPA-free for safety. Mason jars are especially useful for storing salads and dressings.

9. SPOONS AND SPATULAS

These versatile tools are perfect for mixing, stirring, and scraping every last bit of dressing and ingredients from your bowls and containers. Wooden spoons are gentle on your cookware, ensuring you don't scratch your mixing bowls. Silicone spatulas are heat-resistant and flexible, making them ideal for folding ingredients and scraping down the sides of your bowls. And don't forget a good whisk for blending dressings and sauces smoothly.

10. KITCHEN SCALE

When it comes to precise measurements, a kitchen scale is incredibly useful, especially for layers like fruits, nuts, seeds, grains, and proteins. It's particularly helpful if you're tracking portions or following a specific diet. Weighing proteins like chicken, fish, or tofu, helps keep portions consistent, which is key for balanced bowls. It's also great for portioning nuts and seeds, preventing you from accidentally adding too much.

Storing and Packing Your Bowls

Now that you have the right kitchen tools at your disposal, let's move on to another essential part of the bowl-building process: storing and packing your bowls. Much of the problem of food waste lies in improper storage and packing methods.

How many times have you prepared a salad only to find it wilted and soggy by the time you're ready to eat? Or maybe you've noticed your ingredients losing their flavor after just a couple of days? Perhaps you've struggled with keeping your prepped layers organized?

You can easily avoid these common issues with the right storage strategies. Here are some tips and tricks for ensuring your bowls stay fresh, flavorful, and ready to enjoy.

USE AIRTIGHT CONTAINERS

Whether you store your layers in plastic or glass containers, the key to maximum freshness is ensuring they're airtight.

Plastic containers typically have snap-on lids that create a tight seal, preventing air from getting in and causing ingredients to spoil. But they can retain odors, which might affect flavors.

On the other hand, glass containers with airtight seals preserve taste and quality without absorbing odors or stains. Plus, they allow you to see what's inside, serving as a visual reminder of what's prepped and ready to use.

You might consider using plastic containers for layers like grains that don't have strong odors and glass for veggies and dressings. Ultimately, the best choice depends on your personal preferences and needs.

BATCH PREP FOR CONVENIENCE

When it comes to bowl building, batch prepping is a game changer! It'll save you time and ensure you always have fresh layers on hand. Spend a couple of hours at the beginning of the week chopping veggies, cooking starches, and portioning out proteins, then store your layers in separate airtight containers.

Hardy vegetables (carrots, bell peppers, broccoli), starches (beans, rice, pasta) and proteins (chicken, fish, tofu) are perfect for advance prep. However, delicate items like avocado, tomatoes, and fresh herbs are best left until you're ready to eat.

And don't forget the dressings! Whip up batches of your favorites and store them in small mason jars or dressing containers. Most dressings will keep in the fridge for up to a week, ensuring you can quickly build your bowls without daily prep. If your dressing separates, just give it a good shake. For thicker dressings, like those made with tahini or yogurt, stir in a splash of water to smooth them out.

LAYER BOWLS FOR FRESHNESS

In addition to batch prepping, packing whole bowls is an incredibly convenient option. When packing bowls, the way you layer your ingredients is key to keeping everything fresh.

Start with the heaviest ingredients at the bottom, such as proteins. Grains, while somewhat absorbent, also work well near the bottom as they can help manage moisture without becoming soggy. Next, add your chopped veggies and fruits. Delicate greens and herbs should go on top. To avoid soggy salads, keep the dressing separate until you're ready to eat. When layered this way, most salads will stay fresh in the fridge for up to five days.

The process for packing thick-sauced, bound salads like tuna salad and chicken salad, and slaws like coleslaw or broccoli slaw is much simpler. These can be stored whole with the dressing mixed in. As long as the containers are sealed tight, these salads can stay fresh in the fridge for three to five days.

EXPERIMENT WITH MASON JARS

Mason jars are excellent containers for storing salads. They're airtight, portable, fun to fill, and look pretty in the fridge. You can build all the recipes in this book using mason jars. They'll keep all your salad layers fresh until you're ready to enjoy them.

The layering method for mason jars is a bit different. It's best to start with the dressing at the bottom, then add hardy veggies like carrots, bell peppers, and broccoli, followed by grains and proteins. Finally, top it off with delicate ingredients like greens and fruits.

Depending on your eating style, you can use either a 16-ounce or 32-ounce (473-ml or 946-ml) jar. With proper layering, most mason jar salads will stay fresh in the fridge for up to five days. Just make sure your lids are tightly sealed.

LABEL AND DATE YOUR CONTAINERS

Have you ever reached for a container in the fridge and wondered, "How long has this been here?" Labeling and dating your containers eliminates the guesswork, ensuring you use the oldest ingredients first.

Simply use a dry-erase marker or labels to jot down the contents and the date you prepped them. If you find that you've prepped more than you can use in a few days, don't hesitate to freeze some of your ingredients. Just be sure to relabel and date them.

KEEP EVERYTHING COOL

This final tip might seem obvious, but it's worth emphasizing. To maintain freshness, always store your prepped layers and salads in the fridge until you're ready to eat. If you're taking a whole salad to work or on the go, use an insulated lunch bag with an ice pack to keep it chilled. This keeps your ingredients fresh and ensures they stay safe to eat. No one likes a warm, soggy salad!

Also, be mindful of your fridge temperature. Keeping it at or below 40°F (4°C) helps prevent bacterial growth, ensuring your ingredients stay crisp, flavorful, and safe. Consider investing in a fridge thermometer. It's a small tool that can make a big difference in maintaining the perfect storage conditions.

Bringing It All to the Bowl

We've covered a lot of ground in this chapter, but it all starts and ends with the Build Your Bowl system. I've designed this system to make whole food eating simple, straightforward, sustainable, and fun.

Each layer in your bowl has a purpose, from providing essential nutrients, to adding vibrant flavors and textures. So, when you follow this system, I encourage you to understand the balance each layer brings and keep learning how every ingredient nourishes your body. Appreciate the benefits and the calories they bring, rather than agonizing over counting them.

My goal is for you to feel more comfortable and confident about choosing healthy foods and prepping wholesome meals in your own unique way and I'm not just talking about salads. The Build Your Bowl system is about embracing a holistic approach to food, where every layer and every step contributes to your overall well-being.

In the next chapter, we'll explore how to incorporate whole food nutrition into your entire lifestyle. This is just the beginning of your journey to making healthy eating a sustainable habit.

2

Going Beyond the Bowl

In chapter 1, we explored the basics of my Build Your Bowl system. But the overall purpose of the system goes beyond simply making and enjoying delicious salads. It's to help you form a deeper connection with your food, appreciating the nutrients each layer brings and cultivating lifelong healthy eating habits. While this book is packed with nutrient-dense recipes to get you started, my goal in writing this book is to fully equip you with the knowledge and tools to maintain a balanced, nutritious diet that supports your overall wellness.

In this chapter, we'll discuss how mindful eating can deepen your appreciation for the layers in your bowl. We'll also explore practical strategies for incorporating whole food nutrition into your daily routine, making it easier to adopt and stick to healthier eating habits. Finally, we'll wrap up with a discussion about building lifelong healthy eating habits, ensuring that the positive changes you make are sustainable and become a permanent part of your lifestyle.

Even if you're already health-savvy or knowledgeable about nutrition, this chapter will offer new insights and practical tips to enhance your journey. Sometimes, it's as simple as focusing on the joy of the food experience or appreciating the subtle flavors and textures in each bite. This perspective helps lead us to a more mindful approach to eating. Embracing the concepts we cover here will help healthy eating become second nature, and you'll be motivated to maintain these habits for the long term.

The Role of Mindfulness in Healthy Eating

You've probably heard the term "mindfulness," right? It's all about living intentionally and bringing your full attention to the present moment. When you bring that concept to your meals, mindful eating is about being present while you eat, appreciating each bite, and truly enjoying the process. It involves embracing the variety of colors, scents, temperatures, textures, and taste sensations of different foods.

Mindful eating can be as simple as admiring the vibrancy of colorful bell peppers, giving your peach a quick sniff, savoring the warmth of freshly cooked grains, relishing the crunchiness of a fresh cucumber, or appreciating the sweetness of a perfectly ripe strawberry. This level of engagement not only makes meals more enjoyable but also enhances your connection to the food you eat.

Eating mindfully means slowing down and thoroughly chewing your food. This practice aids digestion and allows your body to better absorb the nutrients from whole foods. By eating slowly, you'll also start to recognize when you're full, helping you avoid overeating.

Additionally, mindful eating can help you become more aware of emotional triggers that lead to overeating. By focusing on the present moment and your current state of hunger, you can make more conscious decisions about what and when to eat.

When you combine mindful eating with the Build Your Bowl system, you're not just fueling your body, you'll be a more confident eater. You'll start to appreciate foods instead of restricting them. You might even find yourself trying new foods you'd never considered before.

PRACTICAL TIPS FOR MINDFUL EATING

Fundamentally, mindful eating is about being fully engaged in the eating process and paying attention to your body's cues. I've used this approach with clients of all backgrounds and wellness goals to help them develop a more positive relationship with food. The good news is that making mindful eating a part of your daily routine is pretty simple. Here are some practical tips to help you get started:

Set the Scene: Create a calm and pleasant eating environment. Turn off the TV, put away your phone, and focus on your meal. This helps eliminate distractions and allows you to be fully present.

Engage Your Senses: Take a moment to appreciate the aroma, appearance, and texture of your food. Notice the colors, the arrangement, and the variety in your dish. This sensory engagement can enhance your enjoyment of the meal.

Chew Thoroughly: Make a conscious effort to chew your food well. This not only aids digestion but also slows down your eating pace, giving your brain time to register fullness. Aim to chew each bite 20 to 30 times.

Listen to Your Body: Tune in to your body's hunger and fullness cues. Eat when you're hungry and stop when you're satisfied, not stuffed. This helps prevent overeating and supports healthy weight management.

Reflect on Your Meal: After eating, take a moment to reflect on your experience. Are you satisfied? Energized? Did the meal meet your expectations? This simple practice can help you make better food choices in the future.

INTEGRATING MINDFUL EATING WITH THE BUILD YOUR BOWL SYSTEM

While the practical tips just discussed focus on valuing and appreciating the moment-to-moment experience of eating, it's equally important to understand the "why" behind the foods you eat. This is where the Build Your Bowl system comes in.

Remember, the system puts ingredients at the forefront, providing a structured yet flexible approach to creating nutritious meals. By incorporating mindful eating practices, you can deepen your connection to the food you eat and enhance the benefits of whole food nutrition. I call this ingredient-based mindful eating.

By practicing ingredient-based mindful eating, you gain confidence and develop greater control over your eating patterns and food choices. This approach helps you make healthier decisions and fully embrace each ingredient for what it is and the nutritional goodness it brings to your body.

For instance, knowing that avocados, though calorie-rich, are packed with healthy fats can make eating them more satisfying and guilt-free. So, if you feel compelled to whip up a batch of guacamole, embrace it and savor each bite. Make sense?

Here's how you can integrate ingredient-based mindful eating with the Build Your Bowl system:

Plan with Purpose: When planning your meals, think about how each ingredient contributes to your well-being and the overall balance of your diet. Choose a variety of non-starchy veggies, fruits, high-quality proteins, quality fats, and fiber-rich starches to create nutrient-dense dishes. This balance maximizes nutrition and keeps your meals interesting and satisfying.

Prepare with Intention: As you select each ingredient, take a moment to appreciate its unique qualities. Engage with the process as you chop vegetables, cook grains, and marinate proteins. This can make meal prep more enjoyable and less of a chore.

Cook Mindfully: During the cooking process, notice all the smells, sounds, and colors. The sizzle of vegetables in a pan, the vibrant colors of fresh produce, and the aromatic scents of spices can transform meal prep into a sensory-rich, relaxing activity. This mindfulness in cooking heightens your appreciation for the food you are about to eat.

Enjoy the Presentation: Take a few extra minutes to arrange your bowl, plate, or container beautifully. Remember, we eat with our eyes first. Creating a visually appealing dish can stimulate your appetite and make the meal feel more special.

Reflect on Specific Ingredients: After you eat, take a moment to reflect on how the ingredients made you feel. Did they provide the energy you needed? Did they leave you feeling satisfied? Were there standout flavors or textures you particularly enjoyed? Reflecting on these details helps you better understand your body's responses to different foods and refine future meals.

Incorporating Whole Foods into Every Meal

The Build Your Bowl system is designed to nourish your body with wholesome ingredients at any time of day. By using the system, along with the bowl recipes in this book, you can easily mix and match layers from one meal to the next or even transform your bowls into something else entirely!

Whether it's morning, midday, or evening, you have the freedom to break the traditional meal mold and choose foods that truly satisfy you. This approach not only simplifies meal planning and prep, but also keeps your diet exciting and enjoyable.

Here's how to incorporate whole foods into every meal with this flexible approach.

BREAKING THE FAST: **Anytime, Any Food**

When it's time to break your fast, there's no need to stick to traditional breakfast foods. Whether it's morning or noon, kick things off with something that's both nutritious and satisfying. The best part? You can choose what you truly crave even if it's a hearty salad or a protein-packed bowl.

The Seared Salmon and Mixed Berry Salad (page 141) is a great example. With omega-3-rich salmon, antioxidant-packed berries, leafy spinach, and crunchy walnuts, this bowl is not only delicious, but its layers can easily be repurposed for other meals throughout the day. For instance, consider:

Smoothie Bowls: If you're craving something cool and refreshing, smoothie bowls are a great way to mix up your salad ingredients. Simply blend the spinach and berries from the salad with a cup (240 g) of Greek yogurt or a dairy-free alternative for a creamy base. Top it off with the walnuts for added crunch and good quality fat, and sprinkle with chia or flaxseed for extra fiber and nutrients.

Whole-Grain Options: For a warm, savory start to your day, turn your salad leftovers into a filling breakfast. Repurpose the salmon and spinach by wrapping them in a whole-grain tortilla with a dollop of avocado or hummus for a protein-packed meal. You can also use the greens and salmon in a savory quinoa breakfast bowl topped with a poached egg for added richness and protein.

Salads for Breakfast: Who says you can't enjoy a salad for breakfast? The Seared Salmon and Mixed Berry Salad (page 141) itself makes for a light yet satisfying morning option, with high-quality lean protein, quality fats, and fresh produce that will keep you full for hours. If you prefer a plant-based twist, simply swap the salmon for tofu or tempeh while keeping the vibrant berries and greens for a refreshing, energizing start. For something heartier, try the Sunrise Quinoa Bowl with Scrambled Tofu (page 135). The roasted sweet potatoes and quinoa provide lasting energy, while the protein-rich tofu ensures you're fueled and ready to take on the day.

MIDDAY MEALS: **Flexible and Balanced**

For your midday meal, it's all about keeping your energy levels steady without feeling weighed down. Opt for nutrient-dense dishes that are light but balanced. The Vegan Cobb Salad with Tempeh Bacon (page 106) and the

Eat-the-Rainbow Cobb Salad (page 69) are perfect examples, offering a blend of flexibility and variety while providing all the essential nutrients you need to power through the rest of your day.

Even better, the versatile layers in these bowls can be repurposed for other meals, keeping things exciting. Some examples follow.

Grain Bowls: Looking for a heartier lunch option? Build a grain bowl using layers from the Eat-the-Rainbow Cobb Salad (page 69). Start with a base of whole grains like barley or farro, then add the red cabbage, bell peppers, and tomatoes. Top it with seasoned chicken or chickpeas for protein, and finish with a drizzle of the honey mustard dressing from the recipe or another flavorful dressing from this book. Don't forget to add seeds or nuts for extra crunch and healthy fats.

Wraps and Pitas: Need something portable and quick? Repurpose the ingredients from the Vegan Cobb Salad (page 106) into a whole-grain wrap or pita pocket. Just fill the wrap or pita pocket with tempeh bacon, mixed greens, avocado, and chickpeas for a protein-packed option that's both satisfying and nutritious. Add a spoonful of hummus or guacamole to enhance the flavors even more.

Mason Jar Salads: Take the Eat-the-Rainbow Cobb Salad (page 69) and layer it in a mason jar for an easy lunch on the go. Start with the dressing at the bottom, then add heartier ingredients like bell peppers, red cabbage, and tomatoes. Top with greens and finish with the seasoned chicken or chickpeas. If you prefer the Vegan Cobb Salad (page 106), follow the same layering method using tempeh bacon, avocado, and chickpeas for a plant-based option. This makes for a convenient, healthy lunch that's perfect for busy days.

VERSATILE DINNERS: **Nourishment Without Boundaries**

When dinner rolls around, there's no need to stick to a strict plan. The Build Your Bowl system is all about flexibility, and that extends to dinnertime too. Whether you're craving something light or hearty, the ingredients from the recipes in this book give you endless possibilities.

Take the layers from a salad you loved earlier in the day and turn them into a completely different, satisfying dish by dinnertime. Let's explore a few simple ways to use those same wholesome ingredients to create flavorful, filling dinners with ease.

Stir-Fries: If you're in the mood for a warm, flavorful dinner, stir-fries are a quick and easy way to transform your bowl ingredients into something new. Take the Grilled Chicken and Zucchini Noodles Bowl (page 115) as inspiration. You can sauté zucchini noodles with bell peppers and mushrooms, then add grilled chicken or even shrimp for protein. Toss everything in the lemon-garlic dressing from the recipe for a bright, zesty finish. And it doesn't stop there. Stir-fries are endlessly customizable. Just swap in your favorite vegetables or proteins, and you've got a nourishing dinner on the table in no time.

Sheet Pan Meals: When you want a hands-off approach to dinner, sheet pan meals are always a win. They're easy to prep, require minimal cleanup, and deliver big on flavor. For a simple yet satisfying dinner, use the Hearty Roasted Veggie and Lentil Bowl (page 98) as your guide. Toss vegetables like sweet potatoes, Brussels sprouts, and red onions with olive oil, garlic, and your favorite seasonings, then roast them to perfection. Add cooked lentils and brown rice for a boost of plant-based protein. For extra flavor, drizzle on the tahini dressing from the recipe once everything is out of the oven. It's as simple and delicious as that!

Hearty Soups and Stews: For a comforting, nutrient-dense dinner, soups and stews are the perfect way to take your salad ingredients beyond the bowl. Take inspiration from the Spaghetti Squash and Meatball Bowl (page 125) in this book. Start by combining the roasted spaghetti squash with the meatballs and toss in vegetables like tomatoes, spinach, and carrots. After that, pour in chicken, vegetable, or beef broth until everything is just covered. Let it all simmer together, allowing the flavors to meld into a rich, wholesome meal. It's the ideal choice for chilly evenings or whenever you need something cozy and filling.

NUTRITIOUS SNACKS: **Anytime Energy Boosts**

Snacking doesn't have to be an afterthought. It actually plays an important role in staying energized and satisfied between meals. Whether you're looking for something quick to grab, or a snack to keep you going through a busy day, go with whole foods every time!

Fortunately, the recipes in this book offer plenty of inspiration for creating delicious, nourishing, snacks with ease.

Veggies and Hummus: When you're craving something crunchy and flavorful, a classic combo like veggies and hummus is always a win. Take a cue from the Garden-Fresh Veggie and Hummus Bowl (page 53) for a snack that's both fresh and filling. Pair sliced cucumbers, bell peppers, and carrots with a spoonful of creamy hummus for a nutrient-dense snack rich in fiber, vitamins, and quality fats.

Nuts and Seeds with Fruit: For a grab-and-go snack, nuts and seeds are hard to beat. A small handful of almonds, walnuts, or sunflower seeds, provides a satisfying mix of protein, fats, and fiber to keep you fueled between meals. You can get creative by making your own trail mix with nuts and dried fruits like cherries or raisins. For an extra boost of texture and flavor, sprinkle mixed nuts onto the Light and Crisp Kale Apple Slaw (page 50), which already includes pepitas, adding even more crunch and nutrition to this vibrant salad.

Simple Snack Salads: Turning your meal-size salads into snack-size portions is an easy way to stay energized throughout the day. Leftovers from recipes like the Creamy Broccoli Bliss Bowl (page 57) and Ginger Brussels Sprout Slaw (page 152) can double as refreshing, nutritious snacks. These salads store well, so you can enjoy them straight from the fridge for a light, satisfying snack without extra prep. Just portion out smaller servings, and you'll always have a quick, wholesome bite ready when hunger strikes.

Tailoring Your Meals to Fit Your Preferences

Remember, the Build Your Bowl system is all about flexibility, giving you the freedom to customize your meals to fit your unique dietary needs and personal tastes. Whether you're managing food sensitivities, following a specific diet, or just want to try new flavors, the system adapts easily to your lifestyle. It's about making your meals work for you while still enjoying a balanced mix of nutrients and flavors.

Even small ingredient adjustments can make a big difference in the balance and enjoyment of your meals. For example, if you're avoiding gluten, swap wheat-based grains for options like quinoa or millet. If dairy isn't part of your diet, try using nutritional yeast or vegan cheese instead of traditional cheese. These simple swaps help you keep your meals exciting while staying aligned with your dietary goals.

To make this process easier, the table on page 40 provides a handy guide to common ingredient swaps for different dietary categories. This guide allows you to modify your bowls without sacrificing taste or nutrition. So go ahead! Experiment, get creative and have fun tailoring your bowls to suit your needs.

Building Lifelong Healthy Eating Habits

Healthy eating is about making small, sustainable changes that fit your lifestyle. Think of it as a journey, not a destination, and a way to nourish your body and relationship with food. The tips and strategies we covered in chapter 1 and throughout this chapter are just the beginning. The real key to success lies in consistency and adaptability.

By embracing a flexible approach to eating and making mindful, intentional, food choices, you'll be well on your way to maintaining a balanced, nutritious, diet that supports your overall wellness.

When you make healthy eating a sustainable and enjoyable part of your daily routine, it becomes second nature. Focusing on whole foods, following the Build Your Bowl system, and practicing mindful eating all make it easier and more fun to stick to your goals.

Here are some strategies to help you build and maintain lifelong healthy eating habits that actually stick:

1. EMBRACE VARIETY

Keep your meals exciting and nutritionally balanced by including a wide range of whole foods. Experiment with different fruits, vegetables, proteins, legumes, and grains, like those we covered in chapter 1, to discover new flavors and textures. This variety not only makes your meals more enjoyable but also ensures you get a broad spectrum of nutrients.

2. PLAN AHEAD

Taking the time to plan your meals and snacks can make a huge difference in your eating habits. Set aside time each week to prepare a meal plan, create a shopping list, and prep ingredients. Having healthy options readily available makes it easier to make nutritious choices, even on those busy days.

3. LISTEN TO YOUR BODY

Pay attention to your hunger and fullness cues. Eat when you're hungry and stop when you're satisfied. This mindful approach to eating helps prevent overeating and promotes a healthier relationship with food. Remember, it's okay to indulge occasionally. The key is balance and moderation.

TABLE 3 : COMMON INGREDIENT SWAPS FOR MEAL PREP		
Category	**Ingredient**	**Swap**
Gluten-Free	Wheat-based whole grains	Quinoa, buckwheat, corn, flax, millet, natural rice
	Croutons	Roasted chickpeas, crispy quinoa, gluten-free croutons
	Soy sauce	Tamari, coconut aminos, liquid aminos
	Bread crumbs	Crushed gluten-free crackers, certified gluten-free whole oats
Dairy-Free	Cheese	Nutritional yeast, vegan cheese*
	Cream-based dressings	Cashew cream, avocado-based dressing
	Yogurt or sour cream–based dressings	Unsweetened almond yogurt,* coconut yogurt,* pea yogurt
	Feta cheese	Marinated tofu feta, almond cheese*
Vegan & Vegetarian	Animal-based proteins	Tofu, tempeh, marinated seitan
	Mayonnaise or cream-based dressings	Mashed avocado, tahini, hummus
	Dairy cheese	Vegan cheese,* nutritional yeast
	Pure honey	Pure maple syrup, coconut nectar, agave nectar
Low-Carb	Bread crumbs	Crushed pork rinds, ground flaxseed, almond flour
	Sugar and sweeteners	Monk fruit sweetener, stevia, erythritol, allulose (check labels for low-carb or zero-calorie versions)
	Rice	Cauliflower rice, shredded cabbage
	Pasta	Zucchini noodles (zoodles), shirataki noodles
	Potatoes	Mashed cauliflower, turnips

TABLE 3 : COMMON INGREDIENT SWAPS FOR MEAL PREP		
Category	**Ingredient**	**Swap**
Soy-Free	Soy sauce	Coconut aminos, Worcestershire sauce, soy-free tamari
	Tofu or tempeh	Seitan, chickpeas, lentils combined with grains like rice or quinoa for a complete protein, mushrooms for flavor and texture
	Miso	Chickpea miso, seaweed paste
	Soy milk	Pea milk, hemp milk, almond milk*
Oil-Free	Mayonnaise or cream-based dressings	Mashed avocado, tahini, hummus (blend avocado or tahini with lemon juice)
	Salad toppings	Fresh herbs, citrus juice
	Roasting vegetables	Citrus juice, balsamic vinegar
	Sautéing vegetables	Low-sodium vegetable broth, water
Peanut- & Tree Nut-Free	Whole nuts	Sunflower seeds, pumpkin seeds/pepitas
	Nut-based dressings	Sunflower seed butter, soy nut butter
	Almonds or cashews	Toasted seeds, roasted chickpeas
	Peanut butter	Sunflower butter, tahini
General	Fresh herbs, 1 tablespoon	Dried herbs, 1 teaspoon
	Butter	Ghee, coconut oil
	Broth	Water with a pinch of salt, bouillon cube or paste
	Cooking oil	Avocado oil, ghee, olive oil

** These ingredients do not contain significant amounts of protein, so they may not be suitable substitutes when protein content is important.*

4. EDUCATE YOURSELF

Understanding the nutritional value of the foods you eat can empower you to make healthier choices. Take the time to learn about different nutrients and their benefits. The information we covered in chapter 1 is a great start! Building your knowledge can motivate you to incorporate more nutrient-dense foods into your diet and avoid less healthy options.

5. MAKE HEALTHY EATING ENJOYABLE

Healthy eating shouldn't feel like a chore. Find joy in selecting, preparing, and eating your meals. Try new recipes, explore different cuisines, and involve your family in meal preparation. Even when dining out, aim to make healthy choices enjoyable. By making healthy eating fun and satisfying, you increase the likelihood of sticking with it.

6. STAY HYDRATED

I can't emphasize enough the importance of drinking enough water throughout the day to stay hydrated. Proper hydration aids digestion, supports nutrient absorption, and helps maintain your energy levels. Sometimes, thirst can be mistaken for hunger, leading to unnecessary snacking. Keep a water bottle with you at all times and make it a habit to drink regularly. Enjoying water-rich foods, like cucumbers and melons, can also help you stay hydrated.

7. SET REALISTIC GOALS

Set achievable goals for your eating habits and overall health. Whether it's incorporating more vegetables into your meals, reducing your intake of processed foods, or cooking at home more often, setting realistic goals can help you stay motivated and track your progress.

8. PRACTICE SELF-COMPASSION

Building lifelong healthy eating habits is a journey with ups and downs. Be kind to yourself and recognize that perfection isn't the goal. If you have an off day or make choices that aren't aligned with your goals, don't be too hard on yourself. Learn from the experience and move forward with a positive mindset.

9. SEEK SUPPORT

Having a support system can make a real difference in maintaining healthy eating habits. Share your goals with friends or family members, join a health-focused community or seek guidance from a nutrition professional. Surrounding yourself with supportive people can provide encouragement and accountability.

10. KEEP LEARNING AND ADAPTING

Your body's needs and your lifestyle will evolve over time. Stay open to learning and adapting your eating habits as necessary. Keep exploring new foods, recipes, and nutritional information to ensure your diet remains balanced and enjoyable.

Bringing It All Together

In this chapter, we've explored the importance of whole foods for overall wellness, practical ways to incorporate them into every meal, and how mindful eating can transform your approach to nutrition. Building on the foundational elements we discussed earlier, these strategies will help you create a balanced, nutrient-dense diet that fits your lifestyle.

Remember, healthy eating is a journey, not a destination. With the Build Your Bowl system at your disposal and the tools and knowledge you've gained here, you're well-equipped to make sustainable, enjoyable choices that nourish your body and enrich your relationship with food.

Now, it's time to put these concepts into practice with the delicious, nutrient-packed recipes in the following chapters. Get ready to build some wholesome bowls that not only taste amazing but support your journey toward lifelong wellness. Embrace the flavors, experiment with ingredients, and savor each bite as you continue building a healthier, happier you.

3

Effortless No-Cook & Easy Prep Bowls

We all have those days when cooking feels like too much of a hassle. That's when this collection of no-cook, easy prep bowls comes to the rescue. These recipes are designed to be quick, effortless, and packed with flavor, proving that you don't need complicated techniques to create a nourishing, satisfying meal.

In this chapter, you'll discover a variety of bowls that come together in 30 minutes or less, relying on raw vegetables, pantry staples, and simple proteins that can be prepped in advance.

From the vibrant and Zesty Lemon Pepper Chickpea Salad (page 46) to the herb-packed Radiant Green Goddess Salad (page 64), every recipe offers its own unique twist. You'll experience a playful mix of flavors and textures, like my Quick and Easy Grilled Cheese Salad (page 61), which turns a classic comfort food into a fun, healthy bowl, or the bold and smoky Spicy Chipotle Elote Shrimp Salad (page 54) that brings a burst of Mexican-inspired flavor without much prep.

For days when you want a protein boost, the Hearty Bison Taco Salad Bowl (page 62) offers a satisfying, flavorful option. On the lighter side, the Light and Crisp Kale Apple Slaw (page 50) pairs crunchy kale and apples with pepitas for a refreshing, tangy bite that's perfect as a main or a side dish.

Whether you're preparing for a busy week or just need a quick, energizing meal, these bowls deliver convenience without compromising on taste or nutrition.

Zesty Lemon Pepper Chickpea Salad

This heart-healthy bowl brings together perfectly seasoned chickpeas, crisp vegetables, creamy avocado, and fresh herbs for a refreshing lunch or light dinner.

YIELD: 4 servings • **PREP TIME:** 10 minutes • **COOK TIME:** 20 minutes • **TOTAL TIME:** 30 minutes

FOR THE LEMON PEPPER CHICKPEAS:

1 can (15 ounces, or 425 g) chickpeas (garbanzo beans), drained, rinsed, and patted dry
2 tablespoons (30 ml) fresh lemon juice
1 tablespoon (15 ml) avocado oil
1 teaspoon dried oregano
½ teaspoon smoked paprika
½ teaspoon garlic powder
½ teaspoon dried dill
½ teaspoon cayenne pepper (optional)
½ teaspoon lemon zest
1 tablespoon (8 g) cornstarch or tapioca flour (optional)
Salt and pepper, to taste

FOR THE ZESTY VINAIGRETTE:

¼ cup (60 ml) avocado oil
3 tablespoons (45 ml) apple cider vinegar
2 tablespoons (30 ml) fresh lemon juice
2 cloves garlic, minced
½ teaspoon dried oregano
¼ teaspoon red pepper flakes
1 teaspoon Dijon mustard (optional)
Salt and pepper, to taste

FOR THE BOWL:

1 large cucumber, cubed
1 yellow bell pepper, diced
½ medium red onion, diced
4 scallions, sliced
1 cup (150 g) cherry tomatoes, halved
¼ cup (15 g) fresh Italian parsley, chopped
¼ cup (38 g) crumbled feta cheese
1 avocado, peeled, pitted, and diced

PREPARE THE CHICKPEAS: Preheat the oven to 400°F (200°C). Remove the loose skins from the chickpeas. Let them sit for 10 to 15 minutes to air-dry completely, which helps them absorb flavors and crisp up. Toss the chickpeas with the lemon juice, avocado oil, and seasonings, then coat with cornstarch and gently toss again. Spread on a parchment-lined baking sheet and roast for 20 to 25 minutes, shaking halfway through, until crispy and golden brown. Set aside to cool slightly.

MAKE THE DRESSING: In a small bowl, shaker, or mason jar, combine all the dressing ingredients. Whisk or shake until well blended.

BUILD THE BOWL: In a large mixing bowl, combine the cucumber, bell pepper, onion, scallions, tomatoes, parsley, and feta cheese. Drizzle with the dressing, then add the avocado, and chickpeas. Toss gently to combine. Enjoy immediately as a refreshing main or side dish.

NOTES

MAKE IT YOUR OWN: Feel free to swap the feta for goat cheese or add some nuts or seeds for extra crunch and more protein. You can also experiment with fresh herbs like basil or cilantro for a flavorful twist.

NUTRITIONAL ANALYSIS

PER SERVING: 380 calories; 26 g fat; 31 g carbohydrates; 9 g dietary fiber; 7 g sugars; 9 g protein

The Build Your Bowl System Profile

- NON-STARCHY VEGETABLES: Cucumber, bell pepper, onions, tomatoes, parsley
- FRUITS: Avocado
- WHOLE FOOD FATS: Avocado, cheese, avocado oil
- HIGH-QUALITY PROTEINS: Cheese
- FIBER-RICH STARCHES: Chickpeas
- FLAVOR ENHANCERS: Parsley, cheese, seasonings, dressing

Not Your Average Tuna Salad

Packed with a unique combination of ingredients like sweet grapes, tart Granny Smith apples, and a tangy Greek yogurt dressing, this light and fresh tuna salad offers a wholesome and refreshing twist on a comfort food classic.

YIELD: 4 servings • **PREP TIME:** 15 minutes • **COOK TIME:** 0 minutes • **TOTAL TIME:** 15 minutes

FOR THE HONEY LEMON YOGURT DRESSING:

¾ cup (180 g) plain Greek yogurt (whole milk or 2% reduced fat)
1 tablespoon (20 g) pure honey, or more to taste
1 tablespoon (15 ml) fresh lemon juice, or more as needed
1 teaspoon Dijon mustard
Salt and pepper, to taste

FOR THE BOWL:

3 cans (5 oz / 140 g, each) albacore tuna, drained
2 celery stalks, diced
½ medium red onion, diced
2 large eggs, hard-boiled and chopped
1 cup (150 g) red grapes, halved
1 Granny Smith apple, cored and diced
2 tablespoons (30 g) sweet pickle relish
1 teaspoon dried dill weed
¼ cup (30 g) toasted walnuts, chopped
1 teaspoon salt, or to taste
½ teaspoon pepper, or to taste

OPTIONAL FOR SERVING:

8 slices whole-grain bread or 4 whole wheat tortillas
Lettuce leaves
Tomato slices
Sliced cucumber

MAKE THE DRESSING: In a small bowl, whisk all the dressing ingredients together until well combined.

BUILD THE BOWL: Place the tuna in a large bowl. Add the celery, onion, eggs, grapes, apple, relish, dill weed, and walnuts. Pour the dressing over the mixture and gently toss to combine. Add water or additional lemon juice, as needed for desired consistency. Season with salt and pepper and toss again until well combined.

SERVE: Divide the salad among four bowls and serve immediately or enjoy as a filling for sandwiches, tortilla wraps, or lettuce wraps.

NOTES

CHOOSING TUNA: Albacore tuna is the preferred choice for this recipe because it has a firmer texture, a milder, less "fishy" flavor, and more omega-3s compared to skipjack (light) tuna, which is typically used in tuna salad.

ADD SOME GREENS: Serve the salad on a bed of butter lettuce, spinach, or mixed greens for a nutrient boost.

ENHANCE THE FLAVOR: Add a splash of hot sauce or a sprinkle of paprika for a spicy kick.

NUTRITIONAL ANALYSIS

PER SERVING: 330 calories; 13 g fat; 24 g carbohydrates; 3 g dietary fiber; 19 g sugars; 30 g protein

The Build Your Bowl System Profile

- **NON-STARCHY VEGETABLES:** Celery, onion
- **FRUITS:** Grapes, apple
- **WHOLE FOOD FATS:** Tuna, walnuts, yogurt
- **HIGH-QUALITY PROTEINS:** Tuna, eggs, yogurt
- **FLAVOR ENHANCERS:** Relish, dressing

Light & Crisp Kale Apple Slaw

Forget the heavy mayo! This crisp and colorful slaw is a fresh twist on traditional coleslaw, featuring antioxidant-rich kale, crunchy cabbage, sweet apple, and the savory, nutty flavor of pepitas.

YIELD: 4 servings • **PREP TIME:** 15 minutes • **COOK TIME:** 0 minutes • **TOTAL TIME:** 15 minutes

FOR THE APPLE CIDER VINAIGRETTE:

¼ cup (60 ml) apple cider or unsweetened apple juice
⅓ cup (80 ml) extra-virgin olive oil
2 tablespoons (30 ml) apple cider vinegar
1 tablespoon (20 g) pure maple syrup
1 tablespoon (11 g) whole-grain mustard
Salt and pepper, to taste

FOR THE BOWL:

8 cups (535 g) finely chopped stemmed kale
¼ head red cabbage, finely chopped or shredded
3 small carrots, shredded
1 medium Opal or other sweet apple, peeled, cored, and shredded
¼ cup (15 g) fresh parsley, finely chopped
¼ cup (40 g) toasted pepitas

MAKE THE DRESSING: In a small bowl, shaker, or mason jar, combine all the dressing ingredients. Whisk or shake until well blended.

BUILD THE BOWL: In a large bowl, toss the kale, red cabbage, carrots, apple, parsley, and pepitas with the dressing until evenly coated.

SERVE: Divide the slaw among four bowls. Serve immediately, either as a light stand-alone dish or as a refreshing side to grilled proteins.

NOTES

ADD SOME PROTEIN: For a more filling meal, top with grilled chicken, salmon, shrimp, tofu, or tempeh.

ENHANCE THE FLAVOR: A sprinkle of fresh herbs like dill or cilantro can add an extra burst of flavor.

CUSTOMIZE THE CRUNCH: Swap the pepitas with toasted nuts or other seeds like sunflower seeds for variety.

NUTRITIONAL ANALYSIS

PER SERVING: 313 calories; 24 g fat; 24 g carbohydrates; 6 g dietary fiber; 13 g sugars; 5 g protein

The Build Your Bowl System Profile

- **NON-STARCHY VEGETABLES:** Kale, cabbage, carrots
- **FRUITS:** Apple
- **WHOLE FOOD FATS:** Olive oil, pepitas
- **FLAVOR ENHANCERS:** Parsley, dressing

Avocado Caprese Salad with White Beans

With layers of creamy avocado, buttery white beans, and fresh arugula, this hearty twist on a classic caprese is packed with healthy fats, protein, and fiber.

YIELD: 4 servings • **PREP TIME:** 15 minutes • **COOK TIME:** 0 minutes • **TOTAL TIME:** 15 minutes

4 cups (80 g) arugula
1 batch Balsamic Vinaigrette (see recipe on page 96)
2 large heirloom tomatoes, sliced into wedges
2 large avocados, peeled, pitted, and cubed
1 can (15 ounces, or 425 g) white beans (cannellini or navy), rinsed and drained
8 ounces (225 g) fresh mozzarella, cubed, or mini mozzarella balls
¼ cup (10 g) fresh basil, roughly chopped
1 tablespoon (9 g) toasted pine nuts or sunflower seeds (optional)

BUILD THE BOWL: In a large bowl, toss the arugula with a drizzle of dressing. Add the tomatoes, avocados, beans, mozzarella, and basil and gently toss to combine. Drizzle more dressing over the salad and toss to coat evenly.

SERVE: For a family-style presentation, sprinkle the layered salad with nuts or seeds. For individual servings, divide the tossed salad among four bowls and add nuts or seeds. Serve immediately.

NOTES

OPTIONAL CAPRESE LAYERING: For a more traditional caprese presentation, arrange slices of avocado, tomato, and mozzarella in alternating layers on a serving platter. Top with white beans, basil, and arugula, then drizzle with the dressing.

KEEP THE AVOCADO FRESH: To prevent browning, squeeze a little lemon or lime juice on the avocado slices before adding them to the salad.

CUSTOMIZE YOUR GREENS: Substitute arugula with baby spinach or mixed greens for a milder flavor.

COMPLETE THE PROTEIN: Create a complete plant-based protein by adding more nuts or seeds, such as almonds, pepitas, or hemp seeds.

NUTRITIONAL ANALYSIS

PER SERVING: 495 calories; 25 g fat; 41 g carbohydrates; 15 g dietary fiber; 6 g sugars; 30 g protein

The Build Your Bowl System Profile

- NON-STARCHY VEGETABLES: Arugula, tomatoes, basil
- FRUITS: Avocado
- WHOLE FOOD FATS: Avocado, cheese, olive oil, nuts or seeds
- HIGH-QUALITY PROTEINS: Cheese
- FLAVOR ENHANCERS: Basil, nuts or seeds, dressing

Garden-Fresh Veggie & Hummus Bowl

This easy-to-build bowl combines fresh spinach and vibrant veggies with savory hummus and creamy tahini dressing for a flavorful, satisfying meal.

YIELD: 4 servings • **PREP TIME:** 20 minutes • **COOK TIME:** 0 minutes • **TOTAL TIME:** 20 minutes

FOR THE HUMMUS TAHINI DRESSING:

½ cup (120 g) hummus
2 tablespoons (30 g) tahini
2 tablespoons (30 ml) fresh lemon juice
1 tablespoon (15 ml) apple cider vinegar
1 tablespoon (15 ml) extra-virgin olive oil
1 clove garlic, minced
2 tablespoons (30 ml) water, or more as needed
Salt and pepper, to taste

FOR THE BOWL:

8 cups (240 g) baby spinach
1 cup (150 g) cherry tomatoes, halved
1 cucumber, seeded and diced
2 bell peppers (red and yellow), cored and thinly sliced
2 medium carrots, shredded
¼ red onion, thinly sliced
½ cup (65 g) Kalamata olives, pitted and sliced
½ cup (120 g) hummus
¼ cup (38 g) crumbled feta cheese (optional)
¼ cup (40 g) toasted pepitas
¼ cup (24 g) fresh mint, finely chopped
¼ cup (15 g) fresh parsley, finely chopped

MAKE THE DRESSING: Combine all the dressing ingredients in a blender or food processor. Start blending on low speed, then gradually increase to high speed until smooth. Alternatively, whisk the ingredients together in a small bowl until well combined. Adjust the consistency with more water if needed, and season with salt and pepper to taste.

BUILD THE BOWL: In a large serving bowl, combine the spinach, tomatoes, cucumber, bell peppers, carrots, onion, and olives. Toss gently to mix the vegetables evenly. Drizzle the dressing over the salad and toss again to ensure everything is well coated.

SERVE: Divide the salad among four bowls. Top each with a dollop of hummus, then sprinkle with feta cheese (if using), pepitas, and herbs. Serve immediately with extra dressing on the side if desired.

NOTES

CHOOSING HUMMUS: For the best flavor and texture, opt for either homemade hummus or a high-quality store-bought option. Look for one with a smooth texture, made with simple, wholesome ingredients, and no added sugars or preservatives.

NUTRITIONAL ANALYSIS

PER SERVING: 340 calories; 21 g fat; 31 g carbohydrates; 8 g dietary fiber; 8 g sugars; 12 g protein

The Build Your Bowl System Profile

- NON-STARCHY VEGETABLES: Spinach, tomatoes, cucumber, bell peppers, carrots, onion
- FRUITS: Olives
- WHOLE FOOD FATS: Olives, hummus, cheese, tahini, olive oil, pepitas
- HIGH-QUALITY PROTEINS: Cheese
- FLAVOR ENHANCERS: Cheese, herbs, dressing

Spicy Chipotle Elote Shrimp Salad

Combining the rich and savory tastes of authentic Mexican street corn, perfectly seasoned shrimp, mixed peppers, and a creamy chipotle sauce, this spicy salad is a dream come true for elote fans.

YIELD: 4 servings • **PREP TIME:** 20 minutes plus 20 minutes to marinate • **COOK TIME:** 10 minutes • **TOTAL TIME:** 50 minutes

FOR THE MARINADE:

1 tablespoon (15 ml) fresh lime juice
2 cloves garlic, minced
1 teaspoon chipotle chili powder
1 teaspoon smoked paprika
½ teaspoon cayenne pepper, or to taste
Salt and pepper, to taste

FOR THE SHRIMP:

1 pound (450 g) large shrimp (13 to 15 count), peeled and deveined
1 tablespoon (15 ml) avocado oil

FOR THE CREAMY CHIPOTLE SAUCE:

½ cup (120 g) plain Greek yogurt (whole milk or 2% reduced fat)
¼ cup (60 g) mayonnaise (regular or plant-based)
1 to 2 tablespoons (15 to 30 g) chipotle peppers (1 to 2) in adobo sauce, minced
1 tablespoon (15 ml) fresh lime juice
1 clove garlic, minced
1 teaspoon pure honey, or more to taste
1 teaspoon coconut aminos
¼ teaspoon smoked paprika
¼ teaspoon ground cumin
Salt and pepper, to taste

FOR THE BOWL:

4 cups (600 g) cooked corn kernels
1 red bell pepper, cored and diced
1 poblano pepper, cored and diced
3 scallions, sliced
¼ cup (32 g) crumbled Cotija cheese, or more to taste
¼ cup (4 g) fresh cilantro, chopped, or more to taste

PREPARE THE MARINADE: Mix the marinade ingredients in a medium bowl.

PREPARE THE SHRIMP: Add the shrimp to the marinade and toss to coat well. Cover and refrigerate for 15 to 20 minutes. Heat a large skillet over medium-high heat, add the oil, and cook the shrimp for 2 to 3 minutes per side until pink and opaque. Remove from the heat and set aside.

MAKE THE SAUCE: Add the sauce ingredients to a blender or food processor. Start at low speed and gradually increase the speed until smooth. Adjust the seasoning to taste.

BUILD THE BOWL: In a large bowl, combine the corn, bell pepper, poblano pepper, scallions, Cotija cheese, and cilantro. Pour in the sauce and toss to coat well. Divide among four bowls, top with shrimp, and garnish with additional cilantro and Cotija cheese if desired. Serve immediately.

NOTES

SEAFOOD ALTERNATIVES: Swap shrimp for grilled fish, like salmon or cod, or use grilled scallops.

TIME-SAVING HACK: Use pre-cooked shrimp and pre-shucked corn to cut down on prep. You can also use packaged elote seasoning for a quicker flavor boost.

NUTRITIONAL ANALYSIS

PER SERVING: 440 calories; 20 g fat; 35 g carbohydrates; 5 g dietary fiber; 14 g sugars; 33 g protein

The Build Your Bowl System Profile

- NON-STARCHY VEGETABLES: Bell pepper, poblano pepper, scallions
- WHOLE FOOD FATS: Cheese, avocado oil, yogurt, mayonnaise
- HIGH-QUALITY PROTEINS: Shrimp, cheese, yogurt
- FIBER-RICH STARCHES: Corn
- FLAVOR ENHANCERS: Cheese, cilantro, marinade, sauce

Creamy Broccoli Bliss Bowl

Rich in fiber, antioxidants, and healthy fats, this quick and easy bowl outshines store-bought broccoli salads in both taste and nutrition. Enjoy as a side dish or on a sandwich or make it a full meal by adding more protein.

YIELD: 4 servings • **PREP TIME:** 15 minutes • **COOK TIME:** 5 minutes • **TOTAL TIME:** 20 minutes

FOR THE BOWL:

1 medium head broccoli, chopped into florets (3 to 4 cups, or 255 to 340 g)
¼ medium red cabbage, shredded
2 medium carrots, shredded
½ medium red onion, thinly sliced
1 can (15 ounces, or 425 g) chickpeas (garbanzo beans), drained, rinsed, and patted dry
½ cup (80 g) dried tart cherries
¼ cup (35 g) toasted sunflower seeds
2 or 3 slices bacon, cooked and chopped into bits

FOR THE CREAMY YOGURT VINAIGRETTE:

⅓ cup (80 g) plain Greek yogurt (whole milk or 2% reduced fat)
2 tablespoons (30 ml) extra-virgin olive oil
2 tablespoons (30 ml) apple cider vinegar, or more to taste
1 tablespoon (20 g) pure honey
1 tablespoon (11 g) Dijon mustard
Salt and pepper, to taste

BLANCH THE BROCCOLI: Bring a large pot of salted water to a boil. Fill a large mixing bowl halfway with ice and add cold water, leaving 2 to 3 inches (5 to 8 cm) of space at the top. Add the broccoli florets to the boiling water and blanch for 2 to 3 minutes until they are bright green and tender-crisp. Immediately transfer the broccoli to the ice water to stop the cooking process. Drain well and set aside.

MAKE THE DRESSING: In a small bowl, whisk together the yogurt, olive oil, vinegar, honey, and mustard until smooth. If the dressing is too thick, gradually whisk in 1 to 2 tablespoons (15 to 30 ml) of water or additional vinegar until it reaches your desired consistency. Season with salt and pepper to taste.

BUILD THE BOWL: In a large bowl, combine the broccoli, cabbage, carrots, onion, chickpeas, tart cherries, and sunflower seeds. Drizzle the dressing over the mixture and toss until evenly coated. For the best flavor, let the salad sit for 15 to 20 minutes before serving, or serve immediately if preferred. When ready, divide the salad among four bowls and top each with bacon bits (if using).

NOTES

ADD MORE PROTEIN: Add grilled chicken, beef, or tofu.

ENHANCE THE FLAVOR: Fresh herbs like chives or dill can bring extra freshness to the bowl.

STORING LEFTOVERS: Store any leftovers in an airtight container in the fridge for up to 3 days. For optimal texture, add the bacon just before serving.

NUTRITIONAL ANALYSIS

PER SERVING: 390 calories; 20 g fat; 44 g carbohydrates; 9 g dietary fiber; 23 g sugars; 12 g protein

The Build Your Bowl System Profile

- **NON-STARCHY VEGETABLES:** Broccoli, cabbage, carrots, onion
- **WHOLE FOOD FATS:** Sunflower seeds, bacon, yogurt
- **HIGH-QUALITY PROTEINS:** Bacon, yogurt
- **FIBER-RICH STARCHES:** Chickpeas
- **FLAVOR ENHANCERS:** Cherries, bacon, dressing

Waldorf Salad with a Twist

This flavorful twist on the classic Waldorf salad strikes the perfect balance of rich flavors and contrasting textures, offering a satisfying mix of nutrition and taste.

YIELD: 4 servings • **PREP TIME:** 15 minutes • **COOK TIME:** 0 minutes • **TOTAL TIME:** 15 minutes

FOR THE TANGY YOGURT DRESSING:

¾ cup (180 g) plain Greek yogurt (whole milk or 2% reduced fat)
1 tablespoon (15 ml) fresh lemon juice, or more to taste
1 tablespoon (11 g) Dijon mustard
1 tablespoon (20 g) honey, or more to taste
1 teaspoon apple cider vinegar
¼ teaspoon salt, or to taste
¼ teaspoon pepper, or to taste

FOR THE BOWL:

¾ cup (115 g) red grapes, halved
¾ cup (115 g) green grapes, halved
1 Fuji apple, cored and diced
1 Granny Smith apple, cored and diced
2 celery stalks, thinly sliced
½ cup (60 g) toasted walnuts, chopped
1 avocado, peeled, pitted, and diced
1 head butter lettuce, leaves separated and gently torn
¼ cup (30 g) crumbled blue cheese (optional)

MAKE THE DRESSING: In a small bowl, whisk together the yogurt, lemon juice, mustard, honey, vinegar, salt, and pepper until smooth. Taste and adjust the seasoning, adding a little more lemon juice for extra tang or honey for sweetness, if desired.

BUILD THE BOWL: In a large bowl, gently toss together the grapes, apples, celery, walnuts, and avocado. Drizzle the dressing over the mixture and toss gently to coat all the ingredients without breaking up the avocado. For a flavor boost, let the salad sit for 5 to 10 minutes to allow the flavors to meld.

SERVE: Arrange the torn butter lettuce leaves on individual serving bowls or plates. Top each with a generous portion of the dressed salad. Sprinkle the blue cheese crumbles (if using) over each serving and serve immediately.

NOTES

ADD MORE PROTEIN: Top the salad with grilled chicken, turkey, or roasted chickpeas for a plant-based option.

ENHANCE THE FLAVOR: Sprinkle with smoked paprika, cayenne, or fresh herbs like parsley or tarragon. A drizzle of balsamic glaze or a squeeze of orange juice adds a sweet-tart contrast.

STORING LEFTOVERS: Store the salad ingredients and dressing separately. Build the bowl and toss with dressing just before serving to keep it fresh. The salad will keep for 1 day, and the dressing for up to 3 days.

NUTRITIONAL ANALYSIS

PER SERVING: 360 calories; 20 g fat; 37 g carbohydrates; 7 g dietary fiber; 26 g sugars; 11 g protein

The Build Your Bowl System Profile

- NON-STARCHY VEGETABLES: Lettuce, celery
- FRUITS: Grapes, apples, avocado
- WHOLE FOOD FATS: Avocado, walnuts, cheese, yogurt
- HIGH-QUALITY PROTEINS: Cheese, yogurt
- FLAVOR ENHANCERS: Cheese, dressing

Middle Eastern Tabbouleh Bowl

Inspired by traditional Middle Eastern flavors, this grain-based bowl is packed with fresh herbs, protein-rich quinoa, and nutty chickpeas for a hearty, delicious meal.

YIELD: 4 servings • **PREP TIME:** 15 minutes • **COOK TIME:** 15 minutes • **TOTAL TIME:** 30 minutes

FOR THE BOWL:

½ cup (85 g) quinoa
1 cup (240 ml) water or low-sodium vegetable broth
2 cups (120 g) fresh parsley, finely chopped
½ cup (48 g) fresh mint, finely chopped
2 medium Roma tomatoes, seeded and diced
1 large cucumber, diced
¼ cup (40 g) finely diced red onion
¼ cup (38 g) feta cheese, crumbled (optional)
1 can (15 ounces, or 425 g) chickpeas, rinsed, drained, and patted dry
2 tablespoons (20 g) hemp seeds or pistachio nuts, chopped

FOR THE LEMON TAHINI DRESSING:

¼ cup (60 ml) extra-virgin olive oil
3 tablespoons (45 ml) fresh lemon juice
1 tablespoon (15 g) tahini
1 clove garlic, minced
1 teaspoon lemon zest
¼ teaspoon paprika
1 teaspoon ground cumin
1 teaspoon pure honey or maple syrup
1 tablespoon (15 ml) water, as needed
Salt and pepper, to taste

COOK THE QUINOA: Rinse and drain the quinoa. Combine with the water in a medium saucepan. Bring to a boil, then reduce to a simmer. Cover and cook for 15 to 20 minutes, or until the liquid is absorbed. Fluff with a fork and set aside to cool.

MAKE THE DRESSING: Combine all the dressing ingredients in a small bowl and whisk until smooth. Add water as needed to thin the dressing to your preferred consistency. Season with salt and pepper to taste.

BUILD THE BOWL: In a large bowl, combine the parsley, mint, tomatoes, cucumber, onion, and feta cheese (if using). Add the cooled quinoa and chickpeas, then pour the dressing over the salad. Toss to coat. Garnish with hemp seeds or pistachio nuts. Serve immediately or refrigerate until ready to serve.

NOTES

CUSTOMIZE YOUR GREENS: If you prefer a lesser amount of herbs, reduce the amount of parsley and mint and toss in some arugula or spinach for a milder flavor.

BOOST THE PROTEIN: Add grilled chicken, lamb, or tofu for a more protein-packed bowl.

ENHANCE THE FLAVOR: Roast the chickpeas for extra crunch. Toss with olive oil, cumin, paprika, and salt, then roast at 400°F (200°C) for 20 to 25 minutes, shaking halfway through.

NUTRITIONAL ANALYSIS

PER SERVING: 470 calories; 25 g fat; 51 g carbohydrates; 11 g dietary fiber; 10 g sugars; 16 g protein

The Build Your Bowl System Profile

- NON-STARCHY VEGETABLES: Parsley, mint, tomatoes, cucumber, onion
- WHOLE FOOD FATS: Seeds or nuts, olive oil, tahini
- HIGH-QUALITY PROTEINS: Quinoa, cheese
- FIBER-RICH STARCHES: Quinoa, chickpeas
- FLAVOR ENHANCERS: Cheese, seeds or nuts, dressing

Quick & Easy Grilled Cheese Salad

Featuring high-quality cheese and a tangy tomato vinaigrette, this salad delivers all the rich, savory, goodness of a classic grilled cheese sandwich, with an added boost of protein, fiber, and healthy fats.

YIELD: 4 servings • **PREP TIME:** 15 minutes • **COOK TIME:** 10 minutes • **TOTAL TIME:** 25 minutes

FOR THE BOWL:

8 ounces (225 g) Halloumi cheese, sliced into ½-inch (1 cm)-thick pieces
1 tablespoon (15 ml) extra-virgin olive oil
8 cups (160 g) arugula
1 cup (150 g) grape tomatoes, halved
1 medium English cucumber, diced
1 small red onion, chopped or diced
1 avocado, peeled, pitted, and sliced
¼ cup (10 g) fresh basil, chopped

FOR THE TANGY TOMATO VINAIGRETTE:

1 medium tomato, quartered
3 tablespoons (45 ml) extra-virgin olive oil
2 tablespoons (30 ml) white wine vinegar
1 tablespoon (11 g) Dijon mustard
2 teaspoons pure honey
1 clove garlic, minced
1 tablespoon (2 g) fresh basil, chopped
1 to 2 tablespoons (15 to 30 ml) water, as needed
Salt and pepper, to taste

GRILL THE HALLOUMI: Preheat a grill pan or non-stick skillet over medium heat. Lightly brush the Halloumi slices with olive oil. Grill for 2 to 3 minutes on each side, or until golden brown and slightly crispy. Remove from the heat.

MAKE THE DRESSING: Combine all the dressing ingredients in a blender or food processor. Blend on low speed, gradually increasing the speed until smooth. Add water as needed for your desired consistency and adjust the seasoning as needed to taste.

BUILD THE BOWL: In a large serving bowl, combine the arugula, tomatoes, cucumber, and onion. Drizzle with the dressing and toss gently to coat the vegetables evenly. Divide the salad among four bowls, then top each with grilled Halloumi slices, avocado, and a sprinkle of basil. Serve immediately with extra dressing on the side, if desired.

NOTES

HALLOUMI SUBSTITUTES: If you can't find Halloumi cheese, "grilling cheese" is a great alternative with similar taste and texture. You can also use paneer, queso panela, or even grilled tofu for a different flavor profile.

NUTRITIONAL ANALYSIS

PER SERVING: 450 calories; 37 g fat; 13 g carbohydrates; 4 g dietary fiber; 7 g sugars; 17 g protein

The Build Your Bowl System Profile

- NON-STARCHY VEGETABLES: Arugula, tomatoes, cucumber, onion
- FRUITS: Avocado
- WHOLE FOOD FATS: Cheese, avocado, olive oil
- HIGH-QUALITY PROTEINS: Cheese
- FLAVOR ENHANCERS: Basil, dressing

Hearty Bison Taco Salad Bowl

Loaded with protein-packed bison, fresh veggies, and fiber-rich starches, all topped with a zesty salsa yogurt dressing, this nutrient-dense taco salad bowl is as filling as it is flavorful.

YIELD: 4 servings • **PREP TIME:** 10 minutes • **COOK TIME:** 20 minutes • **TOTAL TIME:** 30 minutes

FOR THE TACO SEASONING:
1 tablespoon (8 g) chili powder
1 teaspoon smoked paprika
1 teaspoon onion powder
1 teaspoon garlic powder
1 teaspoon ground cumin
½ teaspoon pepper
½ teaspoon salt
¼ teaspoon cayenne pepper (optional)
¼ teaspoon red pepper flakes (optional)

FOR THE BISON:
1 pound (450 g) ground bison
Prepared taco seasoning mix, 1 tablespoon (5 g) set aside

FOR THE SALSA YOGURT DRESSING:
½ cup (120 g) salsa (homemade or store-bought)
½ cup (115 g) plain Greek yogurt (whole milk or 2% reduced fat)

FOR THE BOWL:
8 cups (400 g) chopped romaine lettuce
2 cups (300 g) grape tomatoes, halved
4 scallions, sliced
1 cup (150 g) corn, cooked
1 cup (150 g) black beans, drained and rinsed
½ cup (75 g) black olives, sliced
1 avocado, peeled, pitted, and diced
1 jalapeño pepper, thinly sliced (optional)
¼ cup (4 g) fresh cilantro, chopped
¼ cup (30 g) shredded sharp cheddar cheese
Corn tortilla strips, for garnish (optional)

MAKE THE TACO SEASONING: In a small bowl, mix the taco seasoning. Set aside 1 tablespoon (5 g).

COOK THE BISON: Heat a large skillet over medium heat and cook the bison until browned, 7 to 10 minutes. Drain any excess fat, then return the skillet to the heat. Add the taco seasoning and ¼ cup (60 ml) water to the bison, stirring to coat the meat evenly. Let simmer for 2 to 3 minutes until the seasoning is fully absorbed. Remove from the heat and set aside.

MAKE THE DRESSING: Combine all the dressing ingredients, including the reserved taco seasoning, in a blender or food processor. Start on low speed and gradually increase the speed until smooth. Alternatively, whisk the ingredients together in a small bowl until well combined.

BUILD THE BOWL: In a large bowl, toss the lettuce with half of the dressing. Add the tomatoes, scallions, corn, beans, olives, avocado, jalapeño (if using), and cilantro. Toss gently to combine. Divide the salad among four bowls, then top each with bison, cheese, and optional tortilla strips. Drizzle with the remaining dressing and serve immediately.

NOTES

TIME-SAVING HACK: Use pre-washed, pre-chopped lettuce, and canned corn and beans to save time. Use store-bought salsa and shredded cheese to simplify prep.

NUTRITIONAL ANALYSIS

PER SERVING: 465 calories; 21 g fat; 38 g carbohydrates; 13 g dietary fiber; 9 g sugars; 37 g protein

The Build Your Bowl System Profile

- NON-STARCHY VEGETABLES: Lettuce, tomatoes, onions, jalapeño, cilantro
- FRUITS: Avocado
- WHOLE FOOD FATS: Cheese, yogurt
- HIGH-QUALITY PROTEINS: Bison, cheese, yogurt
- FIBER-RICH STARCHES: Corn, beans
- FLAVOR ENHANCERS: Cheese, seasoning mix, dressing

SUNKISSED
SUNKISSED

Radiant Green Goddess Salad

Loaded with kale, broccoli, edamame, and a creamy herb and almond dressing, this refreshing twist on the classic favorite will make you feel radiant inside and out. Toasted spiced seeds and nuts add good crunch, while spiralized zucchini keeps it light and perfectly balanced.

YIELD: 4 servings • **PREP TIME:** 15 minutes • **COOK TIME:** 5 minutes • **TOTAL TIME:** 20 minutes

FOR THE TOASTED NUTS AND SEEDS:

1 tablespoon (15 ml) extra-virgin olive oil
2 tablespoons (20 g) pepitas
2 tablespoons (15 g) almonds, chopped
½ teaspoon smoked paprika
½ teaspoon ground cumin
Salt, to taste

FOR THE CREAMY HERB AND ALMOND DRESSING:

¼ cup (65 g) almond butter
¼ cup (60 ml) fresh lemon juice
2 tablespoons (30 ml) apple cider vinegar
½ avocado, peeled and pitted
1 clove garlic, minced
¼ cup (15 g) fresh parsley
¼ cup (4 g) fresh cilantro
¼ cup (10 g) fresh basil or (24 g) mint
2 tablespoons (30 ml) water, as needed
1 teaspoon miso paste (optional)
Salt and pepper, to taste
1 tablespoon (6 g) lemon zest

FOR BOWL:

6 to 8 cups (400 to 535 g) finely chopped stemmed kale
½ large head broccoli, finely chopped (2 cups, or 170 g)
1 zucchini, spiralized into noodles
1 cucumber, diced
½ cup (78 g) shelled edamame, cooked
½ avocado, peeled, pitted, and sliced

TOAST THE SEEDS AND NUTS: Heat a small skillet over medium heat. Add olive oil, then toss in pepitas and almonds. Sprinkle with paprika, cumin, and a pinch of salt. Toast for 3 to 5 minutes, stirring frequently, until fragrant and lightly browned. Remove from heat and let cool.

MAKE THE DRESSING: In a blender or food processor, combine the almond butter, lemon juice, vinegar, avocado, garlic, and herbs. Blend on low speed, gradually increasing the speed until smooth and creamy. Add water to thin as needed. Optionally, blend in the miso paste. Season with salt, pepper, and lemon zest.

BUILD THE BOWL: In a large bowl, combine the kale, broccoli, zucchini, cucumber, and edamame. Drizzle with dressing and toss to coat evenly. Divide among four bowls, topping each with avocado and the spiced seed and nut blend. Season with salt and pepper to taste. Serve immediately.

NOTES

BOOST THE PROTEIN: Add grilled chicken, tofu, or tempeh for a protein-packed bowl.

SWAP THE GREENS: Substitute kale with spinach, arugula, or mixed greens for a milder flavor.

NUTRITIONAL ANALYSIS

PER SERVING: 310 calories; 23 g fat; 22 g carbohydrates; 8 g dietary fiber; 5 g sugars; 12 g protein

The Build Your Bowl System Profile

- NON-STARCHY VEGETABLES: Kale, broccoli, zucchini, cucumber
- FRUITS: Avocado
- WHOLE FOOD FATS: Avocado, olive oil, almond butter, pepitas, almonds
- HIGH-QUALITY PROTEINS: Edamame
- FLAVOR ENHANCERS: Herbs, spices, dressing

Deconstructed Reuben Salad

A fresh and nutritious twist on the traditional Reuben, this bowl is layered with rich, smoky pastrami, and a medley of veggies like kale, cabbage, and tomatoes, all finished with Swiss cheese and a classic Thousand Island dressing.

YIELD: 4 servings • **PREP TIME:** 20 minutes • **COOK TIME:** 10 minutes • **TOTAL TIME:** 30 minutes

FOR THE THOUSAND ISLAND DRESSING:

½ cup (115 g) plain Greek yogurt (whole milk or 2% reduced fat)
¼ cup (60 g) mayonnaise (regular or plant-based)
¼ cup (60 g) unsweetened ketchup
2 to 3 tablespoons (30 to 45 g) sweet pickle relish
4½ teaspoons (15 g) minced onion
1 clove garlic, minced
1 teaspoon Dijon mustard
1 or 2 teaspoons dried chives
½ teaspoon chili powder
¼ teaspoon sweet paprika
1 teaspoon apple cider vinegar
¼ teaspoon salt, or to taste
2 or 3 drops of hot sauce (optional)

FOR THE BOWL:

6 to 8 cups (400 to 535 g) finely chopped stemmed kale
½ small red cabbage, finely chopped
3 medium carrots, shredded or julienned
1 medium red onion, thinly sliced
1½ cups (225 g) grape tomatoes, halved
10 ounces (285 g) lean beef pastrami, thinly sliced
4 ounces (115 g) shredded Swiss cheese
1 to 2 cups (30 to 60 g) croutons, crushed (optional)

MAKE THE DRESSING: Add all the dressing ingredients to a blender or food processor. Start at a low speed, then gradually increase the speed until the mixture is smooth and well combined.

DRESS THE BASE: In a large bowl, combine the kale and cabbage. Drizzle with about half of the dressing and toss gently to coat evenly. Allow to sit for 5 to 10 minutes to soften the kale and cabbage slightly.

BUILD THE BOWL: Add the carrots, onion, and tomatoes to the dressed kale and cabbage. Toss gently to mix. Top with the pastrami and cheese. Drizzle more dressing over the salad to taste, and toss again gently to ensure everything is evenly coated. Divide the salad among four bowls, top each with crushed croutons (if using), and serve immediately for the best texture and flavor.

NOTES

CUSTOMIZE YOUR PROTEIN: The traditional Reuben is made with corned beef, but beef pastrami has fewer additives and offers richer flavor due to its seasoning and smoking process. Opt for nitrate-free, low-sodium varieties. For a lighter option, try turkey pastrami or roasted turkey breast, which typically has fewer preservatives.

NUTRITIONAL ANALYSIS

PER SERVING: 450 calories; 24 g fat; 30 g carbohydrates; 6 g dietary fiber; 12 g sugars; 30 g protein

The Build Your Bowl System Profile

- **NON-STARCHY VEGETABLES:** Kale, cabbage, carrots, onion, tomatoes
- **WHOLE FOOD FATS:** Cheese, yogurt, mayonnaise
- **HIGH-QUALITY PROTEINS:** Pastrami, cheese, yogurt
- **FIBER-RICH STARCHES:** Croutons
- **FLAVOR ENHANCERS:** Croutons, dressing

Power-Packed High-Protein Bowls

If you're looking to lose weight, build muscle, recover from workouts, or just keep your energy steady throughout the day, protein is a must. But getting enough can sometimes feel repetitive, especially if you're relying on the same go-to meals. That's why this chapter is packed with fresh, flavorful bowls that make it easy (and fun) to get the protein your body needs.

Each of these recipes delivers 20 to 30 grams of protein per serving, helping you mix things up while still hitting your goals. From bold, spicy dishes to comforting, hearty meals, these bowls have something for every craving.

The Caribbean Jerk Chicken Salad (page 79), for instance, features jerk-seasoned chicken paired with fresh veggies and a tangy mango-lime vinaigrette.

For seafood lovers, the Barbecue Pulled Salmon Salad (page 75) offers a smoky, Southern-inspired twist with seasoned salmon and crunchy veggies.

For folks who prefer their protein plant based, the Savory Tofu and Quinoa Salad Bowl (page 73) provides a delicious option with marinated tofu, quinoa, and roasted vegetables.

And for a more indulgent option, try the Deluxe Burger Bowl (page 76), a healthier take on a classic, featuring your favorite burger fixings.

With protein sources ranging from chicken, beef, salmon, shrimp, lamb, and even plant-based options, this chapter ensures you'll never feel stuck in a protein rut.

Eat-the-Rainbow Cobb Salad

With tender chicken, crisp veggies, and a tangy honey mustard dressing, this colorful twist on the classic Cobb delivers a crave-worthy balance of sweet and savory flavors.

YIELD: 4 servings • **PREP TIME:** 20 minutes • **COOK TIME:** 15 minutes • **TOTAL TIME:** 35 minutes

FOR THE CHICKEN:

2 boneless, skinless chicken breasts (about 7 ounces, or 200 g, each)
Salt and pepper, to taste
1 teaspoon garlic powder
1 tablespoon (15 ml) olive oil (optional)

FOR THE HONEY MUSTARD DRESSING:

¼ cup (60 ml) extra-virgin olive oil
2 tablespoons (30 g) plain Greek yogurt (whole milk or 2% reduced fat)
2 tablespoons (40 g) pure honey
2 tablespoons (22 g) Dijon mustard
2 tablespoons (30 ml) apple cider vinegar
1 tablespoon (15 ml) fresh lemon juice
1 teaspoon dried oregano, parsley, or basil
Salt and pepper, to taste

FOR THE BOWL:

8 cups (400 g) chopped romaine lettuce
Salt and pepper, to taste
2 large eggs, hard-boiled and quartered
½ medium red onion, thinly sliced
1 large carrot, shredded
1 yellow bell pepper, cored and diced
1 cucumber, seeded and diced
2 medium vine tomatoes, seeded and diced
¼ small red cabbage, shredded
1 avocado, peeled, pitted, and diced
2 or 3 strips bacon, cooked and chopped (optional)
¼ cup (60 g) crumbled blue cheese (optional)
1 tablespoon (15 g) chopped fresh chives (optional)

COOK THE CHICKEN: Season the chicken breasts with salt, pepper, and garlic powder. Heat a grill pan or non-stick skillet over medium-high heat. If the pan is not non-stick or appears dry, add the olive oil. Cook the chicken for 6 to 7 minutes per side, or until the internal temperature reaches 165°F (74°C). Let it rest for 5 minutes before slicing.

MAKE THE DRESSING: Combine all the dressing ingredients in a blender or food processor. Blend on low speed, gradually increasing the speed until smooth. Alternatively, whisk the ingredients together in a small bowl until well combined.

BUILD THE BOWL: Arrange the lettuce in a large bowl. Season with salt and pepper, drizzle with the dressing, and gently toss the greens to coat evenly. Layer the chicken, eggs, onion, carrot, bell pepper, cucumber, tomatoes, cabbage, and avocado on top of the lettuce in neat sections or rows for a classic Cobb salad presentation.

SERVE: Sprinkle with the bacon, blue cheese, and chives, if desired, and serve family-style with extra dressing on the side.

NOTES

MAKE IT LIGHTER: Reduce or skip the bacon, use only egg whites, and opt for half an avocado. You can also limit or omit the blue cheese.

NUTRITIONAL ANALYSIS

PER SERVING: 540 calories; 33 g fat; 29 g carbohydrates; 7 g dietary fiber; 15 g sugars; 34 g protein

The Build Your Bowl System Profile

- **NON-STARCHY VEGETABLES:** Lettuce, cabbage, carrot, bell pepper, cucumber, tomatoes, onion
- **WHOLE FOOD FATS:** Avocado, bacon, cheese, olive oil, yogurt
- **HIGH-QUALITY PROTEINS:** Chicken, bacon, eggs, yogurt
- **FLAVOR ENHANCERS:** Bacon, cheese, chives, dressing

Mediterranean Shrimp & Pasta Salad

Indulge in the fresh flavors of the Mediterranean with this protein-packed shrimp and pasta salad, inspired by coastal regions where simple, wholesome ingredients shine.

YIELD: 4 servings • **PREP TIME:** 20 minutes • **COOK TIME:** 15 minutes • **TOTAL TIME:** 35 minutes

FOR THE SHRIMP:

14 to 16 ounces (400 to 450 g) shrimp, peeled and deveined
1 teaspoon smoked paprika
½ teaspoon garlic powder
¼ teaspoon red pepper flakes (optional)
1 tablespoon (6 g) lemon zest
Salt and pepper, to taste
Olive oil, for cooking

FOR THE WHITE BALSAMIC VINAIGRETTE:

⅓ cup (80 ml) extra-virgin olive oil
¼ cup (60 ml) white balsamic vinegar
1 tablespoon (20 g) pure honey or maple syrup, or more to taste
1 tablespoon (11 g) Dijon mustard
1 clove garlic, minced
1 teaspoon dried oregano
1 teaspoon dried parsley
Salt and pepper, to taste

FOR THE BOWL:

6 to 8 cups (300 to 400 g) chopped romaine lettuce
1 cup (75 g) whole grain or gluten-free pasta, cooked al dente
¼ medium head red cabbage, shredded
1 cup (150 g) grape tomatoes, halved
1 large cucumber, seeded and cubed
1 orange bell pepper, cored and diced
½ medium red onion, thinly sliced
1 Granny Smith apple, diced
½ cup (75 g) black olives, pitted and sliced
¼ cup (30 g) toasted almonds, chopped or slivered (optional)
¼ cup (38 g) crumbled feta cheese (optional)

COOK THE SHRIMP: In a large bowl, toss the shrimp with the seasonings until evenly coated. Heat a little olive oil in a large skillet over medium heat. Add the shrimp and cook for 2 to 3 minutes per side, or until they turn pink and opaque. Set aside to cool.

MAKE THE DRESSING: In a small bowl, shaker, or mason jar, combine all the dressing ingredients. Whisk or shake until well mixed. Adjust the seasoning to taste.

BUILD THE BOWL: In a large bowl, toss together the lettuce, pasta, cabbage, tomatoes, cucumber, bell pepper, onion, apple, and olives. Drizzle with half the dressing and toss to coat. Divide the salad among four bowls, then top with shrimp, and sprinkle with the optional almonds and feta cheese. Drizzle with more dressing to taste and serve immediately.

NOTES

MAKE IT YOUR OWN: Swap the shrimp for fish, chicken, or tofu. Replace the almonds with walnuts, sunflower seeds, or pepitas.

NUTRITIONAL ANALYSIS

PER SERVING: 490 calories; 27 g fat; 39 g carbohydrates; 9 g dietary fiber; 19 g sugars; 28 g protein

The Build Your Bowl System Profile

- NON-STARCHY VEGETABLES: Lettuce, cabbage, tomatoes, cucumber, bell pepper, onion
- FRUITS: Apple, olives
- WHOLE FOOD FATS: Olives, almonds, olive oil, cheese
- HIGH-QUALITY PROTEINS: Shrimp, cheese
- FIBER-RICH STARCHES: Pasta
- FLAVOR ENHANCERS: Seasonings, dressing, cheese

Pesto Turkey Meatball Bowl

This hearty bowl features juicy, herb-infused turkey meatballs paired with a colorful mix of fresh veggies, tangy sun-dried tomatoes, and finished with a rich basil pesto for nutritious and flavorful meal.

YIELD: 4 servings • **PREP TIME:** 15 minutes • **COOK TIME:** 20 minutes • **TOTAL TIME:** 35 minutes

FOR THE TURKEY MEATBALLS:

1 pound (450 g) ground turkey (93% lean)
¼ cup (30 g) grated Parmesan cheese
2 tablespoons (15 g) flaxseed meal
1 large egg, beaten
2 cloves garlic, minced
2 tablespoons (5 g) fresh basil, chopped
1 tablespoon (4 g) fresh parsley, chopped
½ teaspoon salt, or to taste
¼ teaspoon pepper
1 tablespoon (15 ml) extra-virgin olive oil

FOR THE BASIL PESTO:

¼ cup (10 g) fresh basil leaves
¼ cup (35 g) toasted pine nuts
¼ cup (30 g) grated Parmesan cheese
1 clove garlic, minced
1 tablespoon (15 ml) fresh lemon juice
2 tablespoons (30 ml) extra-virgin olive oil
2 tablespoons (30 ml) water or low-sodium vegetable broth
Salt and pepper, to taste

FOR THE BOWL:

4 cups (80 g) arugula
1 cup (155 g) shelled edamame, cooked
1 medium zucchini, spiralized or thinly sliced
1 medium red bell pepper, thinly sliced
1 medium carrot, shredded
¼ cup (30 g) sun-dried tomatoes, chopped

PREPARE THE MEATBALLS: In a large bowl, combine the ground turkey and meatball seasonings (not including the oil). Mix well and form into 12 evenly sized meatballs. Heat the olive oil in a skillet over medium heat. Cook the meatballs for 10 to 12 minutes, turning occasionally, until browned on all sides and cooked through (internal temperature should reach 165°F/74°C). Set aside.

MAKE THE PESTO: In a blender or food processor, combine the basil, pine nuts, Parmesan cheese, garlic, and lemon juice. Pulse on low speed to combine. While the machine is running, slowly drizzle in the olive oil and water until the mixture becomes smooth and emulsified. Season with salt and pepper to taste.

BUILD THE BOWL: Divide the arugula and edamame among four bowls. Arrange the zucchini, bell pepper, carrot, and sun-dried tomatoes over the greens. Top each bowl with a few turkey meatballs. Drizzle the basil pesto over the meatballs and vegetables. Toss gently to coat everything evenly.

NOTES

SWAPS FOR NUTS: Replace pine nuts with hemp seeds for a similar texture or use sunflower seeds for added crunch.

ENHANCE THE FLAVOR: Sprinkle red pepper flakes over the meatballs, or add a squeeze of lemon juice before serving for extra flavor.

NUTRITIONAL ANALYSIS

PER SERVING: 510 calories; 35 g fat; 14 g carbohydrates; 7 g dietary fiber; 5 g sugars; 37 g protein

The Build Your Bowl System Profile

- NON-STARCHY VEGETABLES: Arugula, zucchini, bell pepper, carrot
- WHOLE FOOD FATS: Olive oil, pine nuts, cheese
- HIGH-QUALITY PROTEINS: Ground turkey, edamame, cheese
- FLAVOR ENHANCERS: Sun-dried tomatoes, cheese, seasonings, dressing

Savory Tofu & Quinoa Salad Bowl

Enjoy this protein-packed, meat-free bowl combining marinated tofu, roasted veggies, tender edamame, and a creamy lemon tahini vinaigrette.

YIELD: 4 servings • **PREP TIME:** 20 minutes plus 30 minutes to marinate • **COOK TIME:** 25 minutes • **TOTAL TIME:** 1 hour 15 minutes

FOR THE TOFU AND VEGETABLES:

1 block (14 to 16 ounces, or 400 to 450 g) organic extra-firm tofu, drained
2 tablespoons (30 ml) low-sodium soy sauce
1 tablespoon (20 g) pure maple syrup
1 tablespoon (15 ml) toasted sesame oil
1 clove garlic, minced
1 teaspoon grated fresh ginger
½ teaspoon smoked paprika
1 tablespoon (15 ml) rice vinegar
1 tablespoon (8 g) cornstarch or tapioca flour (optional)
1 cup (85 g) broccoli florets, chopped
1 orange bell pepper, sliced
1 small red onion, sliced
1 tablespoon (15 ml) extra-virgin olive oil
Salt and pepper, to taste

FOR THE LEMON TAHINI VINAIGRETTE:

⅓ cup (80 g) tahini
3 tablespoons (45 ml) fresh lemon juice
1 to 2 tablespoons (20 to 40 g) pure maple syrup
1 clove garlic, minced
1 teaspoon low-sodium soy sauce
1 tablespoon (15 ml) toasted sesame oil
½ teaspoon ground cumin
2 tablespoons (30 ml) rice vinegar
2 to 3 tablespoons (30 to 45 ml) water, as needed
Salt and pepper, to taste

FOR THE BOWL:

4 cups (600 g) finely chopped stemmed kale
½ cup (85 g) cooked quinoa (red or black)
½ cup (78 g) cooked shelled edamame

PREPARE THE TOFU AND VEGETABLES: Press the tofu following the instructions on page 91, then cut it into cubes. In a medium bowl, whisk together the soy sauce, maple syrup, sesame oil, garlic, ginger, paprika, and vinegar. Add the tofu and toss to coat well. Cover and refrigerate for 30 minutes to 2 hours, then coat with the cornstarch. In a separate bowl, toss the vegetables with olive oil, salt, and pepper.

ROAST THE TOFU AND VEGETABLES: Preheat the oven to 400°F (200°C). Spread the tofu and vegetables on a parchment-lined baking sheet. Roast for 20 to 25 minutes, flipping halfway through until the tofu is golden and crispy, and the vegetables are tender and slightly caramelized.

MAKE THE DRESSING: In a small bowl, shaker, or mason jar, combine all the dressing ingredients, adding water as needed for your desired consistency. Whisk or shake until well mixed.

BUILD THE BOWL: In a large bowl, massage the kale with a drizzle of dressing until softened. Add the quinoa, edamame, roasted vegetables, and tofu. Drizzle with the remaining dressing and serve.

NOTES

ENHANCE THE FLAVOR: Add toasted sesame seeds, fresh herbs, or red pepper flakes.

NUTRITIONAL ANALYSIS

PER SERVING: 490 calories; 29 g fat; 41 g carbohydrates; 8 g dietary fiber; 11 g sugars; 23 g protein

The Build Your Bowl System Profile

- NON-STARCHY VEGETABLES: Kale, broccoli, bell pepper, onion
- WHOLE FOOD FATS: Olive oil, sesame oil, tahini
- HIGH-QUALITY PROTEINS: Tofu, quinoa, edamame
- FIBER-RICH STARCHES: Quinoa
- FLAVOR ENHANCERS: Marinade, dressing

Barbecue Pulled Salmon Salad

Delivering hefty doses of omega-3s, antioxidants, and fiber, this slaw-like salad features perfectly pulled salmon and vibrant veggies, tied together by a smoky barbecue vinaigrette.

YIELD: 4 servings • **PREP TIME:** 20 minutes • **COOK TIME:** 15 minutes • **TOTAL TIME:** 35 minutes

FOR THE BARBECUE SALMON:

1 teaspoon smoked paprika
½ teaspoon garlic powder
½ teaspoon onion powder
½ teaspoon ground cumin
¼ teaspoon pepper
¼ teaspoon dried oregano
⅛ teaspoon cayenne pepper, or to taste
⅛ teaspoon salt, or to taste
4 wild-caught, skinless salmon fillets (about 4 ounces, or 115 g, each)

FOR THE SMOKY BARBECUE VINAIGRETTE:

⅓ cup (80 ml) extra-virgin olive oil
¼ cup (60 ml) apple cider vinegar
2 tablespoons (30 g) unsweetened ketchup
2 teaspoons pure honey
2 teaspoons Dijon mustard
1 teaspoon smoked paprika
1 teaspoon garlic powder
½ teaspoon onion powder
½ teaspoon Worcestershire sauce (optional)
Salt and pepper, to taste

FOR THE BOWL:

8 cups (535 g) finely chopped stemmed kale (red if available)
¼ head red cabbage, shredded
½ small red onion, thinly sliced
1 orange bell pepper, cored and thinly sliced
2 medium carrots, shredded
2 medium vine tomatoes, seeded and diced
4 or 5 radishes, julienned
¼ cup (10 g) fresh dill, chopped

BAKE THE SALMON: Preheat the oven to 375°F (190°C). Combine the salmon seasonings in a small bowl and rub them over the fillets, ensuring they are well coated. Place the salmon on a parchment-lined baking sheet and bake for 12 to 15 minutes, or until the salmon is cooked through and flakes easily with a fork. Let cool slightly, then pull apart into bite-size pieces.

MAKE THE DRESSING: In a small bowl or shaker, combine all the dressing ingredients. Whisk or shake until well mixed. Adjust the seasoning to taste.

BUILD THE BOWL: In a large serving bowl, combine the kale, cabbage, onion, bell pepper, carrots, tomatoes, radishes, and dill. Top with the pulled salmon, drizzle with the dressing, and toss gently to coat. Divide among four bowls and serve immediately, with extra dressing on the side.

NOTES

MAKE IT YOUR OWN: Use the same seasoning blend for proteins like pork, chicken, or tofu. For added crunch, top with toasted nuts or seeds.

NUTRITIONAL ANALYSIS

PER SERVING: 425 calories; 25 g fat; 24 g carbohydrates; 6 g dietary fiber; 11 g sugars; 30 g protein

The Build Your Bowl System Profile

- NON-STARCHY VEGETABLES: Kale, cabbage, onion, bell pepper, carrots, tomatoes, radishes
- WHOLE FOOD FATS: Salmon, olive oil
- HIGH-QUALITY PROTEINS: Salmon
- FLAVOR ENHANCERS: Dill, seasonings, dressing

Deluxe Burger Bowl

Packed with quality protein, healthy fats, and plenty of fresh layers, this bowl has all the classic fixings burger fans love, but over 40 percent fewer calories than a traditional burger and fries!

YIELD: 4 servings • **PREP TIME:** 20 minutes • **COOK TIME:** 15 minutes • **TOTAL TIME:** 35 minutes

FOR THE BURGER MEAT:

1 pound (450 g) ground turkey (93% lean)
1 onion (yellow or white), diced
3 cloves garlic, minced
¾ teaspoon salt, or to taste
¼ teaspoon pepper, or to taste

FOR THE BOWL:

8 cups (400 g) chopped romaine lettuce
1 batch Thousand Island Dressing (see recipe on page 65)
¼ cup (30 g) shredded sharp cheddar cheese
2 cups (150 g) white button mushrooms, diced
1 cucumber, seeded and diced
½ red onion, diced
2 cups (300 g) grape tomatoes, halved
2 or 3 strips bacon, cooked and chopped into bits (optional)
1 to 2 cups (30 to 60 g) croutons, crushed (optional)

COOK THE BURGER MEAT: Add the ground turkey to a hot, lightly greased skillet or pan over medium-high heat. Cook on one side for 1 to 2 minutes, then stir until browned and no pink remains, 7 to 8 minutes. Once browned, stir in the onion, garlic, salt, and pepper.

BUILD THE BOWL: Place the lettuce in a large bowl and drizzle with the dressing, mixing well. Layer on the ground turkey, cheddar, mushrooms, cucumber, onion, and tomatoes. Add more dressing if desired, then top with bacon bits and/or croutons (if using). Serve immediately.

NOTES

CUSTOMIZE YOUR PROTEIN: Ground turkey can be swapped with ground chicken breast (93% lean) or ground beef (93% lean or higher). For a meatless option, use a high-quality meatless ground product.

NUTRITIONAL ANALYSIS

PER SERVING: 525 calories; 32 g fat; 27 g carbohydrates; 6 g dietary fiber; 12 g sugars; 35 g protein

The Build Your Bowl System Profile

- **NON-STARCHY VEGETABLES:** Lettuce, mushrooms, cucumber, onion, tomatoes
- **WHOLE FOOD FATS:** Cheese, bacon, yogurt, mayonnaise
- **HIGH-QUALITY PROTEINS:** Turkey, cheese, bacon, yogurt
- **FLAVOR ENHANCERS:** Bacon, croutons, dressing

Beef & Broccoli Bowl

Tossed in a savory sesame ginger dressing, this protein-packed bowl features tender, marinated beef, crisp broccoli, and a colorful mix of fresh veggies.

YIELD: 4 servings • **PREP TIME:** 15 minutes plus 30 minutes to marinate • **COOK TIME:** 20 minutes • **TOTAL TIME:** 1 hour 5 minutes

FOR THE BEEF:

2 tablespoons (30 ml) low-sodium tamari
1 tablespoon (15 ml) toasted sesame oil, plus 1½ teaspoons
1 tablespoon (15 ml) rice vinegar
1 clove garlic, minced
1 teaspoon finely grated fresh ginger
½ teaspoon mushroom powder
1 pound (450 g) beef sirloin or flank steak, thinly sliced

FOR THE SESAME GINGER DRESSING:

¼ cup (60 ml) low-sodium tamari
1½ teaspoons toasted sesame oil
2 tablespoons (30 ml) rice vinegar
1 tablespoon (15 ml) fresh lemon juice
1 teaspoon tahini (optional for thickening)
1 teaspoon finely grated fresh ginger
½ teaspoon garlic powder
¼ teaspoon red pepper flakes (optional)
2 tablespoons (30 ml) water, as needed
Salt and pepper, to taste

FOR THE BOWL:

1 medium head broccoli, chopped into florets (3 to 4 cups, or 255 to 340 g) and blanched
½ medium head Napa cabbage, shredded
½ medium cucumber, thinly sliced
1 medium red bell pepper, thinly sliced
1 small carrot, julienned
Salt and pepper, to taste
2 scallions, thinly sliced
1 tablespoon (8 g) toasted sesame seeds

PREPARE THE BEEF: Mix the tamari, 1 tablespoon (15 ml) of the sesame oil, vinegar, garlic, ginger, and mushroom powder in a medium bowl. Add the beef and toss to coat well. Cover and refrigerate for 30 minutes to 2 hours. Heat the remaining 1½ teaspoons of sesame oil in a large skillet over medium-high heat. Stir-fry the beef for 4 to 5 minutes until browned and cooked through. Transfer to a plate and let cool slightly.

MAKE THE DRESSING: In a small bowl, whisk together the dressing ingredients until well mixed. Add water as needed for your desired consistency. Season with salt and pepper.

BUILD THE BOWL: In a large bowl, combine the broccoli, cabbage, cucumber, bell pepper, and carrot with salt, pepper, and a light drizzle of the dressing. Toss to ensure an even coating.

SERVE: Divide the salad among four bowls. Top with the beef and drizzle with more dressing. Garnish with scallions and sesame seeds. Serve immediately or refrigerate for up to 2 hours for a chilled salad.

NOTES

MAKE IT YOUR OWN: Swap beef for chicken, shrimp, or tofu. Add red pepper flakes or a squeeze of lemon or lime juice for extra flavor. You can also top with slivered almonds or crushed peanuts for crunch.

NUTRITIONAL ANALYSIS

PER SERVING: 310 calories; 13 g fat; 17 g carbohydrates; 4 g dietary fiber; 5 g sugars; 32 g protein

The Build Your Bowl System Profile

- NON-STARCHY VEGETABLES: Broccoli, cabbage, cucumber, bell pepper, carrot
- WHOLE FOOD FATS: Sesame oil
- HIGH-QUALITY PROTEINS: Beef
- FLAVOR ENHANCERS: Scallions, sesame seeds, marinade, dressing

Caribbean Jerk Chicken Salad

This vibrant, nutritious salad brings the bold flavors of the Caribbean to your bowl with spicy jerk-seasoned chicken, fresh veggies, and a tangy mango lime vinaigrette.

YIELD: 4 servings • **PREP TIME:** 20 minutes plus 30 minutes to marinate • **COOK TIME:** 15 minutes • **TOTAL TIME:** 1 hour 5 minutes

FOR THE JERK CHICKEN:

1 tablespoon (15 ml) extra-virgin olive oil
1 tablespoon (15 ml) low-sodium soy sauce
1 tablespoon (15 ml) fresh lime juice
2 cloves garlic, minced
1 teaspoon minced or grated fresh ginger
1 teaspoon ground allspice
1 teaspoon dried thyme
1 teaspoon brown sugar
½ teaspoon cayenne pepper
1 Scotch bonnet or habanero pepper, finely chopped
Salt and pepper, to taste
2 boneless, skinless chicken breasts (about 7 ounces, or 200 g, each)

FOR THE MANGO LIME VINAIGRETTE:

¼ cup (60 ml) extra-virgin olive oil
2 to 3 tablespoons (30 to 45 ml) fresh lime juice, or more to taste
1 tablespoon (20 g) pure honey
1 tablespoon (11 g) Dijon mustard
¼ ripe mango, peeled, pitted, and diced
1 clove garlic, minced
Salt and pepper, to taste

FOR THE BOWL:

8 cups (440 g) chopped leaf lettuce (green or red)
Salt and pepper, to taste
½ red bell pepper, cored and thinly sliced
½ yellow bell pepper, cored and thinly sliced
½ cup (75 g) cherry tomatoes, halved
1 small red onion, thinly sliced
¾ ripe mango, peeled, pitted, and diced
¼ cup (4 g) fresh cilantro, chopped
1 avocado, peeled, pitted, and sliced
¼ cup (34 g) toasted cashews, chopped

PREPARE THE CHICKEN: Mix the olive oil, soy sauce, lime juice, garlic, ginger, allspice, thyme, brown sugar, cayenne, Scotch bonnet, and salt and pepper in a medium bowl, add the chicken, and turn to coat well. Cover and refrigerate for 30 minutes to 2 hours. Preheat a grill, grill pan, or non-stick skillet over medium-high heat. Cook the marinated chicken for 6 to 7 minutes per side until the internal temperature reaches 165°F (74°C). Let rest for 5 minutes before slicing.

MAKE THE DRESSING: Add all the dressing ingredients to a blender or food processor. Start on low speed and gradually increase the speed until smooth. Adjust the lime juice and salt and pepper to taste.

BUILD THE BOWL: In a large bowl, season the lettuce with salt and pepper, drizzle with the dressing, and toss gently. Add the bell peppers, tomatoes, onion, mango, and cilantro, tossing to combine. Divide among four bowls, top with the chicken and avocado, and drizzle with more dressing. Garnish with cashews. Serve immediately.

NOTES

CUSTOMIZE YOUR BOWL: For a smoky twist, grill bell peppers alongside the chicken. For a vegetarian option, substitute the chicken with jerk-marinated tofu or tempeh.

NUTRITIONAL ANALYSIS

PER SERVING: 440 calories; 28 g fat; 25 g carbohydrates; 6 g dietary fiber; 13 g sugars; 27 g protein

The Build Your Bowl System Profile

- NON-STARCHY VEGETABLES: Lettuce, bell peppers, tomatoes, onion
- FRUITS: Avocado, mango
- WHOLE FOOD FATS: Avocado, olive oil, cashews
- HIGH-QUALITY PROTEINS: Chicken
- FLAVOR ENHANCERS: Cilantro, marinade, dressing

Tandoori Chicken & Spiced Cauliflower Bowl

Inspired by Indian flavors, this bowl features tender tandoori-spiced chicken thighs, roasted cauliflower, and crisp veggies, all topped with a creamy cumin-infused yogurt dressing.

YIELD: 4 servings • **PREP TIME:** 15 minutes plus 30 minutes to marinate • **COOK TIME:** 25 minutes • **TOTAL TIME:** 1 hour 10 minutes

FOR THE TANDOORI CHICKEN:

½ cup (115 g) plain Greek yogurt (whole milk or 2% reduced fat)
1 tablespoon (15 ml) fresh lemon juice
1 tablespoon (15 g) tandoori spice mix
1 teaspoon ground cumin
2 cloves garlic, minced
1 teaspoon minced fresh ginger
½ teaspoon salt, or to taste
1 pound (450 g) boneless, skinless chicken thighs

FOR THE SPICED CAULIFLOWER:

1 medium head cauliflower, cut into florets
1 tablespoon (15 ml) extra-virgin olive oil
1 teaspoon ground turmeric
1 teaspoon ground cumin
½ teaspoon ground coriander
¼ teaspoon cayenne pepper (optional)
Salt and pepper, to taste

FOR THE CUMIN-INFUSED YOGURT DRESSING:

½ cup (115 g) plain Greek yogurt (whole milk or 2% reduced fat)
1 tablespoon (15 ml) fresh lemon juice
1 tablespoon (15 ml) extra-virgin olive oil
½ teaspoon ground cumin
Salt and pepper, to taste

FOR THE BOWL:

4 cups (120 g) baby spinach
1 medium cucumber, diced
1 medium red bell pepper, thinly sliced
¼ medium red onion, thinly sliced

PREPARE THE CHICKEN: Mix the the yogurt, lemon juice, spice mix, cumin, garlic, ginger, and salt in a medium bowl. Add the chicken and turn to coat. Cover and refrigerate for 30 minutes to 4 hours. Preheat a grill pan or skillet over medium-high heat. Cook the chicken for 5 to 7 minutes per side, or until the internal temperature reaches 165°F (74°C). Let rest for 5 minutes before slicing.

ROAST THE CAULIFLOWER: Preheat the oven to 400°F (200°C). Toss the cauliflower florets with the olive oil and spices and spread on a baking sheet. Roast for 20 to 25 minutes, tossing halfway through, until golden and tender.

MAKE THE DRESSING: Whisk together all the dressing ingredients in a small bowl.

BUILD THE BOWL: Divide the spinach among four bowls. Arrange the cucumber, bell pepper, and onion on top of the spinach, then drizzle a small amount of dressing over each bowl. Top with the sliced chicken and roasted cauliflower. Drizzle with additional dressing and serve immediately.

NOTES

ENHANCE THE FLAVOR: Top with fresh cilantro or mint for added freshness. Add red pepper flakes for extra heat.

NUTRITIONAL ANALYSIS

PER SERVING: 370 calories; 16 g fat; 23 g carbohydrates; 7 g dietary fiber; 10 g sugars; 35 g protein

The Build Your Bowl System Profile

- NON-STARCHY VEGETABLES: Spinach, cauliflower, cucumber, bell pepper, onion
- WHOLE FOOD FATS: Olive oil, yogurt
- HIGH-QUALITY PROTEINS: Chicken, yogurt
- FLAVOR ENHANCERS: Tandoori marinade, spice blend, dressing

Grilled Peach & Salmon Burrata Bowl

This bright summer bowl pairs sweet grilled peaches and savory salmon with creamy burrata for a perfect balance of flavors and textures.

YIELD: 4 servings • **PREP TIME:** 20 minutes • **COOK TIME:** 15 minutes • **TOTAL TIME:** 35 minutes

FOR THE PEACHES:

2 or 3 ripe peaches, halved and pitted
1 tablespoon (15 ml) extra-virgin olive oil

FOR THE SALMON:

4 wild-caught, skinless salmon fillets (about 4 ounces, or 115 g, each)
1 tablespoon (15 ml) extra-virgin olive oil
Salt and pepper, to taste

FOR THE BALSAMIC REDUCTION:

1 cup (240 ml) balsamic vinegar

FOR THE BOWL:

4 to 6 cups (80 to 120 g) fresh arugula
Salt and pepper, to taste
2 medium heirloom tomatoes, halved or quartered
1 medium cucumber, cut into ribbons using a peeler
4 ounces (115 g) burrata cheese, torn into pieces
¼ cup (35 g) toasted pine nuts
¼ cup (10 g) fresh basil leaves, torn

GRILL THE PEACHES: Preheat a grill or grill pan over medium-high heat. Brush the peach halves with olive oil. Grill the peaches, cut-side down, for 3 to 4 minutes, until grill marks form and the peaches are slightly caramelized. Remove from the grill.

GRILL THE SALMON: Pat the salmon fillets dry and brush with the olive oil. Season with salt and pepper. Place the fillets on the grill and cook for 3 to 4 minutes per side, or until the internal temperature reaches 145°F (63°C) and the flesh flakes easily with a fork. Remove from the grill and let rest for a few minutes.

MAKE THE BALSAMIC REDUCTION: In a small saucepan over medium heat, bring the balsamic vinegar to a gentle simmer. Reduce the heat to low and cook for 10 to 15 minutes, stirring occasionally, until the vinegar thickens to a syrupy consistency and reduces by half. Remove from the heat and let cool slightly.

BUILD THE BOWL: In a medium bowl, season the arugula with salt and pepper and drizzle with a little of the balsamic reduction. Toss gently to coat. Divide the arugula evenly among four serving bowls. Add the tomatoes and cucumber. Top with the grilled peaches, burrata, and the salmon. Sprinkle with the pine nuts and basil. Drizzle additional balsamic reduction over the bowls. Serve immediately.

NOTES

SELECTING PEACHES: Choose peaches that are firm but slightly ripe for grilling. This will help them hold their shape and achieve a beautiful caramelization without becoming too soft.

NUTRITIONAL ANALYSIS

PER SERVING: 450 calories; 24 g fat; 24 g carbohydrates; 3 g dietary fiber; 18 g sugars; 35 g protein

The Build Your Bowl System Profile

- **NON-STARCHY VEGETABLES:** Arugula, tomatoes, cucumber
- **FRUITS:** Peaches
- **WHOLE FOOD FATS:** Salmon, cheese, pine nuts, olive oil
- **HIGH-QUALITY PROTEINS:** Salmon, cheese
- **FLAVOR ENHANCERS:** Balsamic reduction, basil

Lamb Meatball & Sweet Potato Bowl

Inspired by Mediterranean cuisine, in which lamb has been a staple for centuries, this bowl pairs this versatile protein with roasted sweet potatoes, crisp veggies, and refreshing tzatziki.

YIELD: 4 servings • **PREP TIME:** 20 minutes • **COOK TIME:** 30 minutes • **TOTAL TIME:** 50 minutes

FOR THE POTATOES:

2 medium sweet potatoes, peeled and diced
1 tablespoon (15 ml) extra-virgin olive oil
¼ teaspoon ground cinnamon
Salt and pepper, to taste

FOR THE MEATBALLS:

1 pound (450 g) ground lamb
¼ cup (15 g) fresh parsley, chopped
3 tablespoons (30 g) minced yellow onion
2 cloves garlic, minced
1 teaspoon dried oregano
½ teaspoon ground cumin
½ teaspoon salt, or to taste
¼ teaspoon pepper, or to taste

FOR THE MINTY TZATZIKI DRESSING:

1 small English cucumber, grated or minced and drained
½ cup (115 g) plain Greek yogurt (non-fat or 2% reduced fat)
2 tablespoons (30 ml) extra-virgin olive oil
2 tablespoons (12 g) fresh mint, chopped
1 or 2 cloves garlic, minced
1 tablespoon (15 ml) red wine vinegar
1 tablespoon (15 ml) fresh lemon juice
Salt and pepper, to taste

FOR THE BOWL:

8 cups (535 g) chopped Lacinato kale
¼ red onion, thinly sliced
½ cup (75 g) cherry tomatoes, halved

ROAST THE POTATOES: Preheat the oven to 400°F (200°C). Toss the sweet potatoes with the olive oil, cinnamon, salt, and pepper. Spread evenly on a parchment-lined baking sheet. Roast for 20 to 25 minutes, or until tender and slightly caramelized. Set aside. Leave the oven on.

PREPARE THE MEATBALLS: In a large bowl, combine the ground lamb and seasonings until well mixed. Form into 1-inch (2.5 cm) meatballs (20 to 22 total) and place them on a separate parchment-lined baking sheet. Bake for 15 to 20 minutes, or until browned and cooked through to an internal temperature of 160°F (71°C). Remove from the oven.

MAKE THE DRESSING: Add all the dressing ingredients to a blender or food processor, and blend until smooth, starting on low speed and gradually increasing the speed to high. Chill for 20 to 30 minutes for a more refreshing flavor.

BUILD THE BOWL: Arrange the kale in a large serving bowl. Layer with the roasted sweet potatoes, onion, and tomatoes. Top with the lamb meatballs, drizzle with the dressing, and divide among four bowls. Serve immediately with extra dressing on the side.

NOTES

ENHANCE THE FLAVOR: Add fresh herbs like dill or oregano to enhance the bowl's flavor even more.

NUTRITIONAL ANALYSIS

PER SERVING: 530 calories; 37 g fat; 24 g carbohydrates; 5 g dietary fiber; 7 g sugars; 25 g protein

The Build Your Bowl System Profile

- NON-STARCHY VEGETABLES: Kale, onion, tomatoes
- WHOLE FOOD FATS: Olive oil, yogurt
- HIGH-QUALITY PROTEINS: Lamb, yogurt
- FIBER-RICH STARCHES: Sweet potatoes
- FLAVOR ENHANCERS: Seasonings, dressing

Rustic Autumn Chicken Salad

With bold colors, balanced textures, and a blend of sweet, savory, and tangy flavors, this salad captures the essence of fall in a single, flavorful bowl.

YIELD: 4 servings • **PREP TIME:** 20 minutes • **COOK TIME:** 25 minutes • **TOTAL TIME:** 45 minutes

FOR THE POTATOES:

2 medium sweet potatoes, peeled and diced
1 tablespoon (15 ml) extra-virgin olive oil
¼ teaspoon ground cinnamon
Salt and pepper, to taste

FOR THE CHICKEN:

2 boneless, skinless chicken breasts (about 7 ounces, or 200 g, each)
Salt and pepper, to taste
1 teaspoon garlic powder
1 tablespoon (15 ml) extra-virgin olive oil, or as needed

FOR THE MAPLE DIJON VINAIGRETTE:

⅓ cup (80 ml) extra-virgin olive oil
¼ cup (60 ml) apple cider vinegar
2 tablespoons (40 g) pure maple syrup
2 tablespoons (22 g) Dijon mustard
1 or 2 cloves garlic, minced
1 tablespoon (4 g) fresh parsley, finely chopped
Salt and pepper, to taste

FOR THE BOWL:

8 cups (240 g) mixed greens (arugula, spinach, or kale)
Salt and pepper, to taste
1 medium carrot, shredded
½ English cucumber, sliced
½ cup (75 g) grape tomatoes, halved
¼ red onion, thinly sliced
1 medium Fuji or Honeycrisp apple, diced
1 avocado, peeled, pitted, and sliced
¼ cup (30 g) toasted pecans, chopped (optional)
1 tablespoon (4 g) fresh parsley, finely chopped

ROAST THE POTATOES: Preheat the oven to 400°F (200°C). Toss the sweet potatoes with the olive oil, cinnamon, salt, and pepper. Spread them evenly on a parchment-lined baking sheet. Roast for 20 to 25 minutes, or until tender and slightly caramelized. Set aside to cool.

COOK THE CHICKEN: Season the chicken breasts with the salt, pepper, and garlic powder. Heat a grill pan or non-stick skillet over medium-high heat. If the pan is not non-stick or appears dry, add the olive oil. Cook the chicken for 6 to 7 minutes per side, or until the internal temperature reaches 165°F (74°C). Let it rest for 5 minutes before slicing.

MAKE THE DRESSING: In a small bowl, shaker, or mason jar, combine all the dressing ingredients. Whisk or shake until well mixed. Adjust the seasoning to taste.

BUILD THE BOWL: Spread the mixed greens in a large bowl. Season with salt and pepper, drizzle with dressing, and toss the greens to coat evenly. Arrange the sweet potatoes, carrot, cucumber, tomatoes, onion, apple, and chicken on top in sections. Toss everything together if desired or leave as is for an appealing presentation.

SERVE: Add avocado slices, a sprinkle of pecans (if using), and parsley. Serve family-stye with extra dressing on the side.

NOTES

MAKE IT YOUR OWN: This versatile salad can be customized with other seasonal vegetables, fruits, and flavor enhancers to suit your tastes.

NUTRITIONAL ANALYSIS

PER SERVING: 560 calories; 35 g fat; 36 g carbohydrates; 8 g dietary fiber; 16 g sugars; 27 g protein

The Build Your Bowl System Profile

- NON-STARCHY VEGETABLES: Mixed greens, carrot, cucumber, tomatoes, onion
- FRUITS: Apple
- WHOLE FOOD FATS: Avocado, pecans, olive oil
- HIGH-QUALITY PROTEINS: Chicken
- FIBER-RICH STARCHES: Sweet potatoes
- FLAVOR ENHANCERS: Parsley, dressing

5

Vibrant Vegan & Vegetarian Bowls

Eating plant based isn't about relying on imitation products or trying to make vegetables taste like something else. It's about enjoying the unique flavors, textures, and nutrients that whole, plant-based foods bring to the table. This chapter is packed with bowls that showcase the best of what plants have to offer—meals that taste great while providing the protein and essential nutrients your body needs, especially those amino acids that can be challenging to get in a vegan diet.

Each recipe highlights nutrient-dense ingredients, and where possible, incorporates complete proteins to keep your meals balanced and satisfying.

The Sweet Sesame Tofu and Edamame Bowl (page 91), for example, is a flavorful, protein-rich option that'll keep you full and energized throughout the day. For something lighter, try the Pear and Edamame Harvest Salad (page 92), a sweet-and-savory blend that makes for a refreshing, quick lunch.

If you prefer something heartier, the Southwest Farro Bowl (page 93) combines fiber-rich grains for a hearty dish with complete protein. One of my personal favorites is the Rainbow Three-Bean Salad (page 88), featuring a vibrant mix of legumes and fresh veggies for a wholesome, visually appealing meal.

While some recipes include vegetarian ingredients like dairy for added variety, the star of each of bowl in this chapter is the vegetables, fruits, herbs, and other plants that nourish your body and keep you feeling your best. These bowls prove that plant-based eating can be simple, satisfying, and full of flavor.

Rainbow Three-Bean Salad

A great choice for meal prep, this colorful medley of savory beans, fresh vegetables, and herbs balanced with a tangy-sweet dressing makes the perfect nutrient-packed side dish or light main course.

YIELD: 4 servings • **PREP TIME:** 15 minutes • **COOK TIME:** 0 minutes • **TOTAL TIME:** 15 minutes

FOR THE MAPLE BALSAMIC VINAIGRETTE:

¼ cup (60 ml) balsamic vinegar
3 tablespoons (45 ml) extra-virgin olive oil
1 tablespoon (20 g) pure maple syrup
1 teaspoon Dijon mustard
1 clove garlic, minced
¼ teaspoon smoked paprika
Salt and pepper, to taste

FOR THE BOWL:

½ can (7.5 ounces, or 210 g) kidney beans, drained and rinsed
½ can (7.5 ounces, or 210 g) chickpeas (garbanzo beans), drained, rinsed, and patted dry
½ can (7.5 ounces, or 210 g) cannellini beans, drained and rinsed
1½ bell peppers (red, orange, and yellow), cored and diced
2 or 3 Roma tomatoes, seeded and diced
½ English cucumber (with skin), diced
½ small red onion, diced
2 tablespoons (8 g) finely chopped fresh parsley
2 tablespoons (5 g) finely chopped fresh basil
Salt and pepper, to taste
⅛ teaspoon red pepper flakes, or to taste (optional)

MAKE THE DRESSING: In a small bowl, shaker, or mason jar, combine the vinegar, olive oil, maple syrup, mustard, garlic, and paprika. Whisk or shake until well mixed. Season with salt and pepper to taste.

BUILD THE BOWL: In a large mixing bowl, combine the kidney beans, chickpeas, and cannellini beans. Add the bell peppers, tomatoes, cucumber, onion, and herbs. Pour the dressing over the salad and gently toss to ensure all ingredients are evenly coated. Adjust the seasoning with additional salt, pepper, and red pepper flakes, if desired.

SERVE: For best results, refrigerate the salad for at least 30 minutes, or up to 2 hours, to allow the flavors to meld. Enjoy it on its own as a refreshing side dish, or pair it with a high-quality protein. To keep it plant based, serve with tempeh, a slice of crusty whole-grain bread, and a sprinkle of your favorite nuts and seeds for added texture and flavor.

NOTES

COMPLETE THE PROTEIN: While the beans in this salad provide a solid plant-based protein source, they don't form a complete protein on their own. To ensure a well-rounded meal with all the essential amino acids your body needs, consider pairings such as tempeh, nuts, and seeds.

NUTRITIONAL ANALYSIS

PER SERVING: 340 calories; 13 g fat; 45 g carbohydrates; 11 g dietary fiber; 11 g sugars; 13 g protein

The Build Your Bowl System Profile

- **NON-STARCHY VEGETABLES:** Bell peppers, tomatoes, cucumber, onion
- **WHOLE FOOD FATS:** Olive oil
- **FIBER-RICH STARCHES:** Beans
- **FLAVOR ENHANCERS:** Herbs, dressing

Sweet Sesame Tofu & Edamame Bowl

This vegan bowl features a combination of perfectly marinated tofu, buttery edamame, and crisp fresh veggies, all topped with a sweet sesame vinaigrette that's good enough to drink.

YIELD: 4 servings • **PREP TIME:** 30 minutes • **COOK TIME:** 15 minutes • **TOTAL TIME:** 45 minutes

FOR THE SWEET SESAME VINAIGRETTE:

6 tablespoons (90 ml) coconut aminos or low-sodium soy sauce
3 tablespoons (45 ml) rice vinegar
3 tablespoons (45 ml) fresh lime juice
2 tablespoons (30 ml) toasted sesame oil
4½ teaspoons (30 ml) pure maple syrup
1 clove garlic, minced
2 teaspoons grated fresh ginger
⅛ teaspoon red pepper flakes (optional)
Salt and pepper, to taste

FOR THE BOWL:

1 block (14 to 16 ounces, or 400 to 450 g) organic extra-firm tofu
1 tablespoon (8 g) cornstarch or tapioca flour (optional)
8 cups (160 g) arugula
1 red bell pepper, cored and sliced
¼ head red cabbage, shredded
1 medium carrot, shredded
3 scallions with tops and bulbs, sliced
1 cup (155 g) cooked shelled edamame
Salt and pepper, to taste
½ cup (60 g) toasted cashews
1 tablespoon (9 g) sesame seeds (optional)
½ cup (8 g) fresh cilantro, parsley, or basil, chopped

MAKE THE DRESSING: In a small bowl, whisk all the dressing ingredients together until well combined. Adjust the seasoning to taste. This dressing doubles as a marinade for the tofu.

PREPARE THE TOFU: Drain and press the tofu for 15 to 20 minutes using a press or by placing a towel and a heavy object on top. Cut the tofu into cubes and place them in a medium bowl with a lid, or a resealable bag. Add half the dressing and marinate for 30 minutes to 2 hours. Remove the tofu from the marinade, transfer it to a clean medium bowl, and toss with cornstarch, if desired, for added crispiness. Cook in a non-stick skillet over medium heat until golden, 12 to 15 minutes. Remove and set aside.

BUILD THE BOWL: In a large bowl, combine the arugula, bell pepper, cabbage, carrot, scallions, and edamame. Toss with the dressing, salt, and pepper. Divide among four bowls. Top with tofu, more dressing if desired, cashews, sesame seeds (if using), and herbs. Serve immediately.

NOTES

SOY ALTERNATIVES: Swap out tofu for non-soy tempeh (try a chickpea-based one), seitan, chickpeas, mushrooms, or another protein of your choice. For edamame, use green peas, fava beans, or snap peas as a soy-free substitute.

NUTRITIONAL ANALYSIS

PER SERVING: 390 calories; 17 g fat; 44 g carbohydrates; 10 g dietary fiber; 16 g sugars; 21 g protein

The Build Your Bowl System Profile

- **NON-STARCHY VEGETABLES:** Arugula, cabbage, bell pepper, carrot, onions
- **WHOLE FOOD FATS:** Cashews, sesame seeds, sesame oil
- **HIGH-QUALITY PROTEINS:** Tofu, edamame
- **FLAVOR ENHANCERS:** Herbs, dressing

Pear & Edamame Harvest Salad

This refreshing, nutrient-packed harvest bowl combines sweet pears with crisp greens, buttery edamame, and a savory champagne vinaigrette for the perfect finish. Topped with creamy goat cheese, crunchy pecans, and pepitas, it delivers a rich, yet balanced, mix of flavors and textures for a hearty lunch or light dinner.

YIELD: 4 servings • **PREP TIME:** 15 minutes • **COOK TIME:** 10 minutes • **TOTAL TIME:** 25 minutes

FOR THE CHAMPAGNE VINAIGRETTE:

3 tablespoons (45 ml) champagne vinegar
2 tablespoons (30 ml) grapeseed oil
2 tablespoons (30 ml) extra-virgin olive oil
1 to 2 tablespoons (20 to 40 g) pure honey or maple syrup
2 cloves garlic, minced
1 small shallot, minced
1 teaspoon fresh thyme leaves, chopped
Salt and pepper, to taste

FOR THE BOWL:

8 cups (440 g) chopped leaf lettuce (green and red)
Salt and pepper, to taste
1 cup (155 g) cooked shelled edamame
2 pears (Bartlett and Red Anjou), cubed
½ small cucumber, thinly sliced
¼ small fennel bulb, shaved
⅓ cup (40 g) toasted pecans, chopped
2 tablespoons (20 g) toasted pepitas
1 tablespoon (10 g) chia seeds
⅓ cup (50 g) crumbled goat cheese

MAKE THE DRESSING: In a small bowl, shaker, or mason jar, combine all the dressing ingredients. Whisk or shake until well mixed. For a creamier consistency, blend the ingredients in a blender or food processor, starting at a low speed and gradually increasing the speed until smooth.

BUILD THE BOWL: In a large bowl, season the leaf lettuce with salt and pepper and drizzle with some of the dressing. Toss to coat the greens evenly. Add the edamame, pears, cucumber, and shaved fennel. Drizzle with additional dressing to taste and gently toss to combine.

SERVE: Divide the salad evenly among four bowls. Top each with toasted pecans, pepitas, chia seeds, and goat cheese. Serve immediately with extra dressing on the side if desired.

NOTES

BOOST THE PROTEIN: For more protein, toss in extra edamame or top the salad with grilled tofu or tempeh for a satisfying, vegetarian-friendly option.

ENHANCE THE FLAVOR: To add extra depth of flavor, try roasting the pears for a caramelized taste or glazing the pecans in honey or maple syrup and cinnamon for a sweet, crunchy addition.

NUTRITIONAL ANALYSIS

PER SERVING: 415 calories; 29 g fat; 28 g carbohydrates; 9 g dietary fiber; 15 g sugars; 13 g protein

The Build Your Bowl System Profile

- **NON-STARCHY VEGETABLES:** Lettuce, cucumber, fennel
- **FRUITS:** Pears
- **WHOLE FOOD FATS:** Pecans, pepitas, chia seeds, cheese
- **HIGH-QUALITY PROTEINS:** Edamame, chia seeds, cheese
- **FLAVOR ENHANCERS:** Cheese, dressing

Southwest Farro Bowl

Vibrant, hearty, and packed with bold Southwestern flavors, this vegan bowl delivers plenty of fiber and complete protein from the trio of farro, corn, and beans, while the roasted vegetables and a zesty cilantro lime dressing bring the dish to life.

YIELD: 4 servings • **PREP TIME:** 20 minutes • **COOK TIME:** 25 minutes • **TOTAL TIME:** 45 minutes

FOR THE CILANTRO LIME DRESSING:

¼ cup (60 ml) extra-virgin olive oil
3 tablespoons (45 ml) fresh lime juice
1 tablespoon (15 ml) apple cider vinegar
1 tablespoon (11 g) Dijon mustard
1 tablespoon (20 g) pure maple syrup
1 or 2 cloves garlic, minced
¼ cup (4 g) fresh cilantro, chopped
1 teaspoon ground cumin
½ teaspoon smoked paprika
Salt and pepper, to taste

FOR THE BOWL:

¾ cup (150 g) farro
1½ cups (360 ml) water or low-sodium vegetable broth
2 medium bell peppers (orange and yellow), cored and diced
1 cup (150 g) cherry tomatoes, halved
1 cup (150 g) cooked corn kernels
1 tablespoon (15 ml) extra-virgin olive oil
Salt and pepper, to taste
6 to 8 cups (400 to 535 g) finely chopped stemmed kale
1 can (15 ounces, or 425 g) black beans, rinsed and drained
4 scallions, sliced
1 avocado, peeled, pitted, and diced
¼ cup (4 g) fresh cilantro, chopped
¼ cup (40 g) toasted pepitas

MAKE THE DRESSING: In a small bowl, shaker, or mason jar, combine all the dressing ingredients. Whisk or shake until well mixed. Adjust the seasoning to taste.

COOK THE FARRO: Rinse the farro and add to a medium saucepan with the water. Bring to a boil, then reduce to a simmer. Cover and cook until tender and the liquid is absorbed, 20 to 25 minutes. Fluff with a fork and set aside.

ROAST THE VEGETABLES: Preheat the oven to 400°F (200°C). Toss the bell peppers, tomatoes, and corn with olive oil, salt, and pepper on a parchment-lined baking sheet. Roast for 15 to 20 minutes until tender and slightly caramelized. Set aside to cool.

BUILD THE BOWL: In a large bowl, toss the kale with a few tablespoons of dressing and massage it gently to soften. Add the farro, vegetables, black beans, scallions, avocado, and cilantro. Toss gently to combine, adding more dressing as needed.

SERVE: Divide the salad among four bowls. Top each with pepitas and drizzle with extra dressing, if desired. Serve immediately.

NOTES

ADD MORE PROTEIN: Toss in spiced tofu or seitan for a protein boost. Grilled tempeh or sautéed chickpeas also complement the flavors in this bowl.

NUTRITIONAL ANALYSIS

PER SERVING: 520 calories; 25 g fat; 64 g carbohydrates; 16 g dietary fiber; 11 g sugars; 18 g protein

The Build Your Bowl System Profile

- NON-STARCHY VEGETABLES: Kale, bell peppers, tomatoes
- FRUITS: Avocado
- WHOLE FOOD FATS: Avocado, olive oil, pepitas
- FIBER-RICH STARCHES: Farro, corn, black beans
- FLAVOR ENHANCERS: Cilantro, dressing

Vibrant Collard & Black-Eyed Pea Salad

If you've never tried raw collard greens, you're in for a treat. Softened by a zesty balsamic vinaigrette, these earthy greens pair beautifully with black-eyed peas and vibrant veggies, making this salad just right for a light lunch or a refreshing side.

YIELD: 4 servings • **PREP TIME:** 35 minutes plus 30 minutes to marinate • **COOK TIME:** 0 minutes • **TOTAL TIME:** 1 hour 5 minutes

8 cups (280 g) collard greens, destemmed and thinly sliced
1 batch Balsamic Vinaigrette (see recipe on page 96)
Salt and pepper, to taste
2 cups (350 g) canned black-eyed peas, drained and rinsed
1½ bell peppers (red, orange, and yellow), cored and diced
1 large cucumber, seeded and diced
2 medium carrots, finely chopped
½ medium red onion, diced
4 scallions, thinly sliced
2 Roma tomatoes, diced
1 or 2 jalapeño peppers, finely chopped (optional)
1 tablespoon (2 g) fresh basil, finely chopped

PREPARE THE COLLARD GREENS: Rinse the collards under cold water, then pat them dry with a clean towel or use a salad spinner to remove excess moisture. In a large bowl, massage the collards with a generous amount of dressing and a pinch of salt for 2 to 3 minutes to soften and enhance their flavor. Let the collards sit for at least 20 to 30 minutes to absorb the flavors and soften. For the best results, marinate them for 1 to 2 hours or even refrigerate overnight.

BUILD THE BOWL: Combine all the salad ingredients in a large mixing bowl, pour over the remaining dressing, and toss well to evenly coat everything. Cover and refrigerate for at least 30 minutes, or up to 2 hours, to allow the flavors to meld. Toss again before serving to redistribute the dressing. Enjoy chilled or at room temperature, either on its own as a refreshing side dish or paired with tofu, tempeh, or a slice of whole-grain bread.

NOTES

MARINATING TIP: Letting the collards sit for 10 minutes (or overnight) after massaging, and chilling the salad for 30 minutes, enhances both flavor and texture.

COMPLETE THE PROTEIN: For a well-rounded meal with all the essential amino acids, try the suggested pairings or add feta, goat cheese, or your favorite nuts and seeds for extra texture and flavor.

NUTRITIONAL ANALYSIS

PER SERVING: 295 calories; 15 g fat; 37 g carbohydrates; 10 g dietary fiber; 13 g sugars; 7 g protein

The Build Your Bowl System Profile

- NON-STARCHY VEGETABLES: Collard greens, bell peppers, cucumber, carrots, onions, tomatoes, jalapeño
- WHOLE FOOD FATS: Olive oil
- FIBER-RICH STARCHES: Black-eyed peas
- FLAVOR ENHANCERS: Basil, dressing

Triple Green Power Bowl

When it comes to green garden salads, the darker the leaves, the more nutrients they contain. This bowl features a powerhouse trio of leaf lettuce, arugula, and dandelion leaves, delivering a cocktail of vitamins and antioxidants to make one of the healthiest garden salads you'll ever eat!

YIELD: 4 servings • **PREP TIME:** 20 minutes • **COOK TIME:** 0 minutes • **TOTAL TIME:** 20 minutes

FOR THE BALSAMIC VINAIGRETTE:

¼ cup (60 ml) extra-virgin olive oil
2 tablespoons (30 ml) balsamic vinegar
2 teaspoons pure maple syrup, or more to taste
2 teaspoons Dijon mustard
1 clove fresh garlic, minced
½ teaspoon dried basil
Salt and pepper, to taste

FOR THE BOWL:

4 cups (220 g) chopped leaf lettuce (green or red)
2 cups (40 g) arugula
2 cups (60 g) dandelion leaves
Salt and pepper, to taste
2 cups (300 g) grape tomatoes, halved
2 medium carrots, peeled and sliced into thin rounds
½ medium red onion, thinly sliced
1 yellow bell pepper, cored and thinly sliced
1 cucumber, thinly sliced
½ cup (75 g) crumbled feta cheese (optional)
1 cup (60 g) croutons (optional)

MAKE THE DRESSING: Add all the dressing ingredients to a blender or food processor. Start at a low speed and gradually increase the speed until smooth. Alternatively, mix the ingredients in a bowl, dressing shaker, or mason jar, and whisk or shake until well-blended.

PREPARE THE GREENS: In a large bowl, combine the leaf lettuce, arugula, and dandelion leaves. Season with salt and pepper. Drizzle the dressing over the greens and toss to coat.

BUILD THE BOWL: Scatter the tomatoes, carrots, onion, bell pepper, and cucumber over the dressed greens. Add more dressing if desired and gently toss. Sprinkle with feta cheese and croutons (if using). Serve immediately.

NOTES

CUSTOMIZE YOUR GREENS: Feel free to substitute other greens like spinach or mixed baby greens to suit your taste.

ADD MORE PROTEIN: For a heartier meal, add grilled chicken, salmon, shrimp, tofu, or tempeh bacon.

BRING THE CRUNCH: If you're skipping the croutons, consider adding nuts or seeds for extra crunch and nutrition.

NUTRITIONAL ANALYSIS

PER SERVING: 300 calories; 20 g fat; 25 g carbohydrates; 4 g dietary fiber; 10 g sugars; 7 g protein

The Build Your Bowl System Profile

- **NON-STARCHY VEGETABLES:** Lettuce, arugula, dandelion leaves, onion, carrots, cucumber, bell pepper, tomatoes
- **WHOLE FOOD FATS:** Cheese, olive oil
- **HIGH-QUALITY PROTEINS:** Cheese
- **FIBER-RICH STARCHES:** Croutons
- **FLAVOR ENHANCERS:** Cheese, croutons, dressing

Hearty Roasted Veggie & Lentil Bowl

Combining roasted vegetables, lentils, and brown rice with an herbaceous lemon tahini dressing, this warm and earthy bowl delivers on heartiness and flavor.

YIELD: 4 servings • **PREP TIME:** 15 minutes • **COOK TIME:** 30 minutes • **TOTAL TIME:** 45 minutes

FOR THE HERBY LEMON TAHINI DRESSING:

⅓ cup (80 g) tahini
2 tablespoons (30 ml) extra-virgin olive oil
2 tablespoons (30 ml) fresh lemon juice
1 tablespoon (15 ml) red wine vinegar
1 to 2 tablespoons (20 to 40 g) pure maple syrup, or to taste
1 teaspoon Dijon mustard
1 clove garlic, minced
1 teaspoon lemon zest
1 tablespoon (4 g) fresh parsley, chopped
1 teaspoon fresh tarragon, chopped (optional)
¼ teaspoon ground cumin
2 tablespoons (30 ml) water, or more as needed
Salt and pepper, to taste

FOR THE BOWL:

2 cups (200 g) Brussels sprouts, halved
1 medium zucchini, sliced or diced
1 large red onion, sliced
1 large sweet potato, cut into ¼-inch (6 mm) cubes
2 tablespoons (30 ml) extra-virgin olive oil
1 teaspoon paprika
½ teaspoon ground cumin
Salt and pepper, to taste
4 cups (120 g) baby spinach
½ cup (90 g) cooked brown rice
½ cup (100 g) cooked brown lentils

MAKE THE DRESSING: In a small bowl, whisk together the tahini, olive oil, lemon juice, vinegar, maple syrup, mustard, garlic, lemon zest, parsley, tarragon (if using), and cumin. Gradually add water until the dressing reaches your desired consistency. Season with salt and pepper. Adjust the sweetness if needed with more maple syrup.

ROAST THE VEGETABLES: Preheat the oven to 400°F (200°C). In a large bowl, toss the Brussels sprouts, zucchini, onion, and sweet potato with the olive oil, paprika, cumin, salt, and pepper. Spread on a baking sheet. Roast for 25 to 30 minutes, tossing halfway through, until golden brown and tender.

BUILD THE BOWL: In a large bowl, gently toss the spinach with half the roasted vegetables. Add the rice and lentils, then top with the remaining vegetables. Drizzle generously with the dressing. Divide the mixture among four bowls, adding more dressing if desired and serve immediately.

NOTES

COMPLETE PROTEIN COMBINATION: Pairing brown rice with lentils creates a complete protein, supplying all nine essential amino acids. That makes this bowl an excellent choice for plant-based eaters looking for a balanced and nutritious meal.

ENHANCE THE FLAVOR: For a flavor boost, cook brown rice and lentils in low-sodium vegetable broth.

LIGHTEN THE CARB LOAD: Reduce the amount of sweet potato or replace it with cauliflower or broccoli. You can also swap some rice for additional greens or bulk it up with low-carb vegetables like spiralized zucchini or carrots.

NUTRITIONAL ANALYSIS

PER SERVING: 505 calories; 26 g fat; 59 g carbohydrates; 9 g dietary fiber; 9 g sugars; 15 g protein

The Build Your Bowl System Profile

- **NON-STARCHY VEGETABLES:** Spinach, Brussels sprouts, zucchini, onion
- **WHOLE FOOD FATS:** Olive oil, tahini
- **FIBER-RICH STARCHES:** Lentils, rice, sweet potato
- **FLAVOR ENHANCERS:** Herbs, spices, dressing

Watermelon & Roasted Beet Salad

This bowl takes watermelon to the next level, pairing its natural sweetness with earthy beets, and creamy goat cheese, all tied together with a rich, herb-infused lemon dressing.

YIELD: 4 servings • **PREP TIME:** 20 minutes • **COOK TIME:** 50 minutes • **TOTAL TIME:** 1 hour 10 minutes

FOR THE HERB-INFUSED LEMON VINAIGRETTE:

¼ cup (60 ml) extra-virgin olive oil
2 tablespoons (30 ml) fresh lemon juice
1 tablespoon (15 g) Greek yogurt or tahini
1 teaspoon Dijon mustard
1 teaspoon pure honey or maple syrup
1 clove garlic, minced
1 tablespoon (4 g) fresh tarragon, finely chopped
1 tablespoon (2 g) fresh basil, finely chopped
Salt and pepper, to taste
1 to 2 tablespoons (15 to 30 ml) water, as needed

FOR THE BOWL:

3 medium beets with tops
1 to 2 tablespoons (15 to 30 ml) extra-virgin olive oil
Salt and pepper, to taste
6 to 8 cups (216 to 288 g) roughly chopped Swiss chard, rinsed
3 cups (450 g) seeded and cubed fresh watermelon
1 small shallot, thinly sliced
⅓ cup (40 g) toasted walnuts, roughly chopped
⅓ cup (50 g) crumbled goat cheese
1 tablespoon (6 g) fresh mint, chopped
1 tablespoon (2 g) fresh basil, chopped
2 teaspoons chia seeds

MAKE THE DRESSING: In a small bowl, whisk together the olive oil, lemon juice, yogurt, mustard, honey, and garlic until smooth. Stir in the tarragon and basil. Season with salt and pepper, and add water to reach your desired consistency.

PREPARE THE BEETS: Trim and set aside the beet greens (you will use these later). Thoroughly rinse, scrub, and dry the beets, then trim the ends and halve them. Preheat the oven to 400°F (200°C). Place the beets in a greased baking dish, drizzle with olive oil, and season with salt and pepper. Cover with foil and roast for 50 to 60 minutes until tender. Let cool, then peel (or leave the skins on), and cube. Set aside.

BUILD THE BOWL: Wash, chop, and dry the beet greens, then combine them with the Swiss chard in a large bowl. Lightly toss the mixed greens with a drizzle of dressing to coat. Add the watermelon, beets, shallot, and toss with more dressing. Divide among four bowls, top with walnuts, goat cheese, herbs, and chia seeds. Serve immediately, with extra dressing on the side if desired.

NOTES

MAKE IT YOUR OWN: Try other leafy greens like spinach or arugula for added variety. Sprinkle in toasted quinoa or edamame for an extra boost of protein and satisfying crunch.

NUTRITIONAL ANALYSIS

PER SERVING: 435 calories; 29 g fat; 38 g carbohydrates; 9 g dietary fiber; 26 g sugars; 11 g protein

The Build Your Bowl System Profile

- **NON-STARCHY VEGETABLES:** Beets with greens, chard, shallot
- **FRUITS:** Watermelon
- **WHOLE FOOD FATS:** Walnuts, cheese, olive oil, chia seeds
- **HIGH-QUALITY PROTEINS:** Cheese, seeds
- **FLAVOR ENHANCERS:** Herbs, seeds, dressing

Tantalizing Tropical Mango-Ginger Tofu Salad

Bring tropical flavors to your bowl with this colorful mix of crisp veggies, sweet mango, and creamy avocado, all paired with irresistible mango-ginger marinated tofu.

YIELD: 4 servings • **PREP TIME:** 30 minutes plus 30 minutes to marinate • **COOK TIME:** 10 minutes • **TOTAL TIME:** 1 hour 10 minutes

FOR THE MANGO-GINGER VINAIGRETTE:

¾ ripe mango, peeled, pitted, and diced
¼ cup (60 ml) toasted sesame oil
¼ cup (60 ml) soy sauce or tamari
2 tablespoons (30 ml) fresh lime juice
2 tablespoons (30 ml) rice vinegar
1 tablespoon (20 g) pure honey or maple syrup
2 teaspoons finely grated fresh ginger
2 cloves garlic, minced
1 teaspoon sriracha (optional)
Salt and pepper, to taste

FOR THE BOWL:

1 block (14 to 16 ounces, or 400 to 450 g) organic extra-firm tofu
1 tablespoon (8 g) cornstarch or tapioca flour (optional)
6 to 8 cups (300 to 400 g) chopped romaine lettuce
1 medium carrot, shredded
¼ head red cabbage, shredded
¼ red onion, thinly sliced
½ English cucumber, sliced
4 or 5 radishes, thinly sliced
2 vine tomatoes, diced
¾ cup (110 g) corn, cooked
½ ripe mango, peeled, pitted, and diced
1 avocado, peeled, pitted, and sliced
Salt and pepper, to taste

MAKE THE DRESSING: Add all the dressing ingredients to a blender or food processor. Start on low speed and gradually increase the speed until smooth. Adjust the seasoning to taste. This dressing also doubles as a marinade for the tofu.

PREPARE THE TOFU: Drain and press the tofu for 15 to 20 minutes using a tofu press or by placing a towel and a heavy object on top. Cut the tofu into cubes and place them in a medium bowl with a lid, or a resealable bag. Add half the dressing and marinate for 30 minutes to 2 hours. Remove the tofu from the marinade, transfer it to a clean medium bowl, and toss with the optional cornstarch for added crispiness. Cook in a non-stick skillet over medium heat until golden, 12 to 15 minutes. Remove and set aside.

BUILD THE BOWL: In a large bowl, toss together the lettuce, carrot, cabbage, onion, cucumber, radishes, tomatoes, and corn. Drizzle with half the dressing and toss to coat. Add the tofu and mango and gently toss to combine. Divide the salad among four bowls, top with avocado, and drizzle with more dressing to taste. Serve immediately, with extra dressing on the side.

NOTES

SOY ALTERNATIVES: Swap out tofu for a non-soy tempeh, chickpeas, or mushrooms.

NUTRITIONAL ANALYSIS

PER SERVING: 430 calories; 25 g fat; 42 g carbohydrates; 10 g dietary fiber; 21 g sugars; 16 g protein

The Build Your Bowl System Profile

- **NON-STARCHY VEGETABLES:** Lettuce, cabbage, tomatoes, carrot, onion, cucumber, radishes
- **FRUITS:** Mango, avocado
- **WHOLE FOOD FATS:** Avocado, sesame oil or olive oil
- **HIGH-QUALITY PROTEINS:** Tofu
- **FIBER-RICH STARCHES:** Corn
- **FLAVOR ENHANCERS:** Dressing

Rubbed Kale Salad with Butternut Squash

Perfect for winter, this salad offers warmth and nutrition to keep you satisfied and energized. The layers of rubbed kale, roasted butternut squash, and quinoa, topped with toasted pecans, pomegranate seeds, and a drizzle of apple cider vinaigrette, showcase the season's best textures and flavors.

YIELD: 4 servings • **PREP TIME:** 20 minutes • **COOK TIME:** 25 minutes • **TOTAL TIME:** 45 minutes

FOR THE APPLE CIDER VINAIGRETTE:

3 tablespoons (45 ml) extra-virgin olive oil
2 tablespoons (30 ml) apple cider vinegar
1 tablespoon (11 g) Dijon mustard
1 tablespoon (20 g) pure maple syrup
1 clove garlic, minced
¼ teaspoon dried oregano
Salt and pepper, to taste

FOR THE BOWL:

2 cups (320 g) diced butternut squash
2 tablespoons (30 ml) extra-virgin olive oil
¼ teaspoon ground cinnamon
⅛ teaspoon ground nutmeg
½ cup (85 g) quinoa (red or black)
1 cup (240 ml) water or low-sodium vegetable broth
8 cups (535 g) chopped stemmed kale
¼ teaspoon salt
½ medium red onion, diced
½ cup (60 g) toasted pecans
½ cup (80 g) fresh pomegranate seeds
½ cup (75 g) crumbled feta cheese (optional)

MAKE THE DRESSING: Add all the dressing ingredients to a small bowl, shaker, or mason jar. Whisk or shake until well blended.

ROAST THE SQUASH: Preheat the oven to 400°F (200°C). Toss the butternut squash with 1 tablespoon (15 ml) olive oil, cinnamon, and nutmeg. Spread on a parchment-lined baking sheet and roast until tender and lightly browned, 20 to 25 minutes.

COOK THE QUINOA: Rinse and drain the quinoa. Add to a medium saucepan with the water. Bring to a boil over medium heat, then reduce the heat, cover, and simmer until the liquid is absorbed, 15 to 20 minutes. Fluff with a fork and set aside to cool.

PREPARE THE KALE: Rinse the kale in cool water, massaging it as you rinse. Drain well. In a large bowl, drizzle the kale with olive oil and sprinkle with salt, then toss and massage for 3 to 5 minutes.

BUILD THE BOWL: Add the butternut squash, and quinoa to the kale. Stir in the dressing and mix well. Top with the onion, pecans, pomegranate seeds, and feta cheese (if using). Serve immediately.

NOTES

ADD MORE PROTEIN: Complete the bowl with grilled chicken, salmon, or tempeh bacon for a protein boost.

NUTRITIONAL ANALYSIS

PER SERVING: 435 calories; 29 g fat; 37 g carbohydrates; 7 g dietary fiber; 10 g sugars; 10 g protein

The Build Your Bowl System Profile

- **NON-STARCHY VEGETABLES:** Kale, onion
- **FRUITS:** Pomegranate seeds
- **WHOLE FOOD FATS:** Olive oil, pecans, cheese
- **HIGH-QUALITY PROTEINS:** Quinoa, cheese
- **FIBER-RICH STARCHES:** Squash, quinoa, dressing
- **FLAVOR ENHANCERS:** Cheese, dressing

Spiced Seitan & Citrus Salad

This vibrant salad features the savory, meaty texture of seitan, complemented by layers of crisp veggies, juicy citrus, and toasted pistachios, all drizzled with a creamy, avocado lemon dressing.

YIELD: 4 servings • **PREP TIME:** 20 minutes • **COOK TIME:** 10 minutes • **TOTAL TIME:** 30 minutes

FOR THE SEITAN:

2 tablespoons (30 ml) extra-virgin olive oil
1 tablespoon (6 g) lemon zest
2 teaspoons smoked paprika
2 teaspoons ground coriander
2 teaspoons dried oregano
¼ to ½ teaspoon red pepper flakes (optional)
Salt and pepper, to taste
16 ounces (450 g) seitan, thinly sliced

FOR THE AVOCADO LEMON DRESSING:

1 avocado, peeled and pitted
2 tablespoons (30 ml) extra-virgin olive oil
2 tablespoons (30 ml) fresh lemon juice
1 tablespoon (15 ml) white wine vinegar
1 tablespoon (20 g) pure maple syrup
1 clove garlic, minced
2 tablespoons (10 g) fresh dill, chopped
1 teaspoon ground cumin
2 to 3 tablespoons (30 to 45 ml) water, as needed
Salt and pepper, to taste

FOR THE BOWL:

6 to 8 cups (330 to 440 g) mixed greens (arugula, spinach, or spring mix)
1 fennel bulb, thinly shaved
1 cucumber, thinly sliced
1 cup (150 g) snap peas, halved
½ red onion, thinly sliced
¼ cup (35 g) pitted green olives, halved
1 orange or grapefruit, peeled and segmented
¼ cup (35 g) toasted pistachios

PREPARE THE SEITAN: Combine the olive oil, zest, herbs, red pepper flakes (if using), and salt and pepper in a medium bowl, add the seitan, and toss until well coated. Let it sit for 10 to 15 minutes. Heat a skillet over medium heat and cook the seitan for 5 to 7 minutes, stirring occasionally, until crispy and golden brown. Set aside.

MAKE THE DRESSING: In a blender or food processor, combine the avocado, olive oil, lemon juice, vinegar, maple syrup, garlic, dill, cumin, salt, and pepper. Blend until smooth, adding water as needed. Adjust the seasoning to taste.

BUILD THE BOWL: In a large salad bowl, add the mixed greens and a drizzle of the dressing. Toss gently to coat. Add the fennel, cucumber, snap peas, and onion, tossing to combine. Divide the salad among four bowls. Top with the seitan, olives, and citrus, then sprinkle with pistachios. Serve immediately with extra dressing on the side.

NOTES

CHOOSING SEITAN: Look for plain or lightly seasoned seitan in the refrigerated section near tofu. Made from wheat gluten, seitan is best classified as a protein but not a complete source. Pairing it with legumes like edamame, chickpeas, or black beans completes its amino acid profile.

NUTRITIONAL ANALYSIS

PER SERVING: 440 calories; 25 g fat; 34 g carbohydrates; 12 g dietary fiber; 13 g sugars; 30 g protein

The Build Your Bowl System Profile

- NON-STARCHY VEGETABLES: Mixed greens, fennel, snap peas, onion
- FRUITS: Citrus, olives, avocado
- WHOLE FOOD FATS: Olives, pistachios, olive oil, avocado
- HIGH-QUALITY PROTEINS: Seitan
- FLAVOR ENHANCERS: Seasonings, dressing

Brussels Sprouts Bowl with Crispy Chickpeas

A go-to when you're craving something warm, this bowl combines roasted Brussels sprouts, cauliflower rice, crispy chickpeas, and balsamic glaze for balanced flavors.

YIELD: 4 servings • **PREP TIME:** 15 minutes • **COOK TIME:** 40 minutes • **TOTAL TIME:** 55 minutes

FOR THE CHICKPEAS:

1 can (15 ounces, or 425 g) chickpeas, drained, rinsed, and patted dry
1 tablespoon (15 ml) extra-virgin olive oil
½ teaspoon smoked paprika
½ teaspoon garlic powder
¼ teaspoon ground cumin
¼ teaspoon ground coriander
Salt and pepper, to taste
1 tablespoon (8 g) cornstarch or tapioca flour (optional)

FOR THE BALSAMIC REDUCTION:

1 cup (240 ml) balsamic vinegar

FOR THE BOWL:

4 to 5 cups (400 to 500 g) Brussels sprouts, halved
2 medium carrots, sliced
1 tablespoon (15 ml) olive oil
Salt and pepper, to taste
4 cups (400 g) cooked cauliflower rice
1 red bell pepper, diced
1 small red onion, thinly sliced
¼ cup (35 g) toasted pine nuts
2 to 3 tablespoons (15 to 25 g) dried cranberries (optional)
2 teaspoons chia seeds
¼ cup (15 g) fresh parsley, chopped

PREPARE THE CHICKPEAS: Preheat the oven to 400°F (200°C). Remove the loose skins by placing the chickpeas on a clean kitchen towel and gently rubbing them. Let air-dry for 10 to 15 minutes to improve crisping. Toss with the olive oil, spices, salt, and pepper. For extra crispiness, add the cornstarch (if using) and gently toss again. Spread on a parchment-lined baking sheet and roast for 20 to 25 minutes, shaking halfway through, until crispy and golden. Set aside. Leave the oven on.

MAKE THE BALSAMIC REDUCTION: Follow the instructions on page 81.

ROAST THE VEGETABLES: Toss the Brussels sprouts and carrots with the olive oil, salt, and pepper. Spread on a baking sheet and roast for 25 to 30 minutes, stirring halfway through, until tender and caramelized. Set aside.

BUILD THE BOWL: In a large bowl, combine the cauliflower rice, Brussels sprouts, carrots, bell pepper, and onion. Toss gently to combine. Divide among four bowls. Drizzle with the balsamic reduction and top with the chickpeas, pine nuts, dried cranberries (if using), chia seeds, and parsley. Serve immediately with extra glaze.

NOTES

MAKE IT YOUR OWN: Swap cauliflower rice with brown rice, barley, or couscous for a different texture. Boost the protein with grilled tofu, tempeh bacon, or edamame.

NUTRITIONAL ANALYSIS

PER SERVING: 405 calories; 18 g fat; 52 g carbohydrates; 13 g dietary fiber; 23 g sugars; 12 g protein

The Build Your Bowl System Profile

- **NON-STARCHY VEGETABLES:** Cauliflower, Brussels sprouts, carrots, bell pepper, onion
- **WHOLE FOOD FATS:** Pine nuts, chia seeds, olive oil
- **HIGH-QUALITY PROTEINS:** Chia seeds
- **FIBER-RICH STARCHES:** Chickpeas
- **FLAVOR ENHANCERS:** Parsley, balsamic reduction, seasonings, dried cranberries, chia seeds

Vegan Cobb Salad with Tempeh Bacon

Packed with crunch and creaminess, this vegan twist on the classic Cobb salad keeps all the flavors you crave without the bacon and eggs.

YIELD: 4 servings • **PREP TIME:** 20 minutes • **COOK TIME:** 20 minutes • **TOTAL TIME:** 40 minutes

FOR THE TEMPEH BACON:

3 tablespoons (45 ml) liquid aminos
3 tablespoons (45 ml) apple cider vinegar
1 to 2 tablespoons (20 to 40 g) pure maple syrup
1 teaspoon smoked paprika
½ teaspoon garlic powder
½ teaspoon black pepper
¼ teaspoon salt
Pinch of cayenne pepper (optional)
8 ounces (225 g) tempeh, cubed or sliced into thin strips

FOR THE LEMON DIJON VINAIGRETTE:

¼ cup (60 ml) extra-virgin olive oil
2 tablespoons (30 ml) fresh lemon juice
1 tablespoon (11 g) Dijon mustard
1 tablespoon (20 g) pure maple syrup
1 teaspoon apple cider vinegar
1 clove garlic, minced
Salt and pepper, to taste

FOR THE BOWL:

8 cups (400 g) chopped romaine lettuce
Salt and pepper, to taste
1 large carrot, shredded
1 medium cucumber, seeded and cubed
1 red bell pepper, cored and diced
½ small red onion, thinly sliced
1 cup (150 g) cherry tomatoes, halved
1 avocado, peeled, pitted, and diced
1 cup (150 g) roasted chickpeas (see page 148)
¼ cup (30 g) toasted walnuts, chopped

PREPARE THE TEMPEH BACON: Whisk together the tempeh seasonings in a small bowl. Heat a non-stick skillet over medium heat, add the tempeh, and pour the seasonings over it. Simmer for 10 minutes, flipping occasionally for even coating. Once the marinade is mostly absorbed, continue cooking for 5 to 7 minutes on each side until browned and slightly crisp. Remove from the heat.

MAKE THE DRESSING: In a small bowl, shaker, or mason jar, combine all the dressing ingredients. Whisk or shake until well mixed, adjusting the seasoning as needed.

BUILD THE BOWL: Arrange the lettuce in a large bowl. Season with salt and pepper, drizzle with dressing, and toss to coat evenly. Layer the carrot, cucumber, bell pepper, onion, tomatoes, and avocado on top of the lettuce in neat sections or rows.

SERVE: Top the salad with tempeh bacon, chickpeas, and walnuts. Serve family-style directly from the large bowl with extra dressing on the side.

NOTES

CHOOSING TEMPEH: Traditional soy-based tempeh is a complete protein. For non-soy options, look for tempeh made from a blend of grains and legumes like brown rice and chickpeas to ensure a complete protein.

NUTRITIONAL ANALYSIS

PER SERVING: 490 calories; 32 g fat; 38 g carbohydrates; 10 g dietary fiber; 13 g sugars; 20 g protein

The Build Your Bowl System Profile

- **NON-STARCHY VEGETABLES:** Lettuce, carrot, cucumber, bell pepper, onion, tomatoes
- **FRUITS:** Avocado
- **WHOLE FOOD FATS:** Avocado, walnuts, olive oil
- **HIGH-QUALITY PROTEINS:** Tempeh
- **FIBER-RICH STARCHES:** Chickpeas
- **FLAVOR ENHANCERS:** Seasonings, dressing

6

Satisfying Low-Carb & Keto Bowls

Cutting back on carbs can make it easy to fall into a routine of boring, flavorless meals. But it doesn't have to be that way! This chapter is all about building hearty, delicious, nutrient-packed bowls that focus on fresh vegetables, high-quality proteins, and healthy fats—no heavy carbs in sight.

The recipes in this chapter swap out high-carb ingredients like pasta and rice for nutrient-rich veggies and other wholesome alternatives.

The Eggplant Parmesan Spinach Salad (page 122), for example, transforms a comfort food classic into a light but filling bowl of tender eggplant and vibrant spinach, topped with a refreshing lemon basil vinaigrette.

If you're craving something savory and bold, the Italian Chopped Salad with Sausage (page 116) brings together juicy sausage, crisp greens, and a medley of vegetables. For a pasta alternative, try the Grilled Chicken and Zucchini Noodles Bowl (page 115), where spiralized zucchini replaces traditional pasta.

Looking for something more adventurous? The Korean Beef Salad with Lettuce Wraps (page 127) features marinated beef, bok choy, and radishes in a creamy miso lime dressing. Seafood lovers will enjoy the Lemon Herb Mahi-mahi Bowl (page 119), with its layers of flaky fish, fiber-rich veggies, and bright citrus notes.

Whether you're following a specific diet or just making healthier choices, this collection of bowls is packed with flavor, variety, and excitement to fit your lifestyle and keep you feeling great.

Savory Sirloin Spring Salad

If you're a meat-and-potatoes kind of person, this salad is a game-changer. Tender sirloin steak, crisp spring mix, and a medley of fresh vegetables come together to create a filling and flavorful meal that's perfectly balanced with lean protein, healthy fats, and gut-friendly fiber.

YIELD: 4 servings • **PREP TIME:** 15 minutes plus 30 minutes to marinate • **COOK TIME:** 10 minutes • **TOTAL TIME:** 55 minutes

FOR THE STEAK:

1 pound (450 g) sirloin steak, trimmed of excess fat
1 teaspoon kosher salt
½ teaspoon pepper
2 cloves garlic, minced
2 tablespoons (8 g) fresh parsley, chopped
1 tablespoon (3 g) fresh thyme leaves
1 tablespoon (4 g) fresh rosemary, chopped
1 tablespoon (15 ml) avocado oil

FOR THE AVOCADO BALSAMIC VINAIGRETTE:

3 tablespoons (45 ml) avocado oil
3 tablespoons (45 ml) balsamic vinegar
1 tablespoon (11 g) Dijon mustard
1 tablespoon (20 g) pure honey
1 clove garlic, minced
1 tablespoon (4 g) fresh parsley, finely chopped
Salt and pepper, to taste

FOR THE BOWL:

8 cups (240 g) spring mix or mixed greens
2 Roma tomatoes, diced
1 cucumber, seeded and diced
1 orange bell pepper, diced
½ red onion, thinly sliced
1 avocado, peeled, pitted, and diced
½ cup (75 g) crumbled feta cheese (optional)

PREPARE THE STEAK: Coat the steak with the seasonings and let sit in the fridge for at least 30 minutes. Heat the avocado oil in a skillet over medium-high heat. Cook the steak for 4 to 5 minutes per side, or until it reaches 140°F (60°C) for medium doneness. Let rest for 5 minutes, then slice thinly against the grain.

MAKE THE DRESSING: Add all the dressing ingredients to a small bowl, shaker, or mason jar. Whisk or shake until well mixed.

BUILD THE BOWL: In a large bowl, combine the spring mix, tomatoes, cucumber, bell pepper, and onion. Toss with the balsamic vinaigrette until the salad is evenly coated. Divide the mixture among four bowls. Top with steak, avocado, and feta cheese (if using). Serve immediately.

NOTES

CUSTOMIZE YOUR PROTEIN: If you don't eat red meat, substitute grilled chicken, salmon, or tofu for a protein-packed alternative.

HERB SUBSTITUTIONS: If fresh herbs aren't available, swap them out for dried ones using a ratio of 1 teaspoon dried for every 1 tablespoon fresh.

NUTRITIONAL ANALYSIS

PER SERVING: 460 calories; 27 g fat; 22 g carbohydrates; 6 g dietary fiber; 12 g sugars; 32 g protein

The Build Your Bowl System Profile

- **NON-STARCHY VEGETABLES:** Spring mix, tomatoes, cucumber, bell pepper, onion
- **WHOLE FOOD FATS:** Cheese, avocado, avocado oil
- **HIGH-QUALITY PROTEINS:** Steak, cheese
- **FLAVOR ENHANCERS:** Cheese, seasonings, dressing

Bacon & Brussels Sprouts Salad Bowl

This colorful, keto-friendly bowl pairs crispy bacon and roasted Brussels sprouts with a wholesome mix of low-carb veggies, delivering bright, bold flavors and satisfying textures.

YIELD: 4 servings • **PREP TIME:** 15 minutes • **COOK TIME:** 25 minutes • **TOTAL TIME:** 40 minutes

FOR THE DIJON VINAIGRETTE:

2 tablespoons (30 ml) extra-virgin olive oil
1 tablespoon (11 g) Dijon mustard
1 tablespoon (15 ml) apple cider vinegar
1 teaspoon fresh lemon juice
½ teaspoon pure maple syrup or honey (optional)
Salt and pepper, to taste

FOR THE BOWL:

1 pound (450 g) Brussels sprouts, trimmed and halved
2 tablespoons (30 ml) extra-virgin olive oil
Salt and pepper, to taste
6 slices cooked bacon, diced
½ avocado, peeled, pitted, and sliced
4 or 5 radishes, thinly sliced
¼ small red cabbage, thinly sliced
½ red bell pepper, thinly sliced
¼ cup (30 g) toasted almonds or pecans, chopped
2 tablespoons (8 g) fresh parsley, chopped (optional)
1 teaspoon red pepper flakes

MAKE THE DRESSING: In a small bowl, whisk together the olive oil, mustard, vinegar, lemon juice, and maple syrup (if using). Season with salt and pepper to taste.

ROAST THE BRUSSELS SPROUTS: Preheat the oven to 400°F (200°C). Toss the Brussels sprouts with olive oil, salt, and pepper. Spread them on a parchment-lined baking sheet and roast for 20 to 25 minutes, stirring halfway through, until golden and crispy. Set aside.

BUILD THE BOWL: Divide the roasted Brussels sprouts among four bowls. Top with bacon, avocado, radishes, cabbage, bell pepper, and nuts. Garnish with parsley (if using) and a sprinkle of red pepper flakes. Drizzle with the dressing and serve immediately.

NOTES

CUSTOMIZE YOUR PROTEIN: For keto-friendly bacon, choose uncured varieties without added sugars, such as nitrate-free or organic options. You can also opt for turkey bacon or other low-carb alternatives to suit your preferences. To boost protein, consider adding a soft-boiled egg, grilled chicken, or turkey to the bowl.

NUTRITIONAL ANALYSIS

PER SERVING: 450 calories; 38 g fat; 19 g carbohydrates; 8 g dietary fiber; 6 g sugars; 12 g protein

The Build Your Bowl System Profile

- NON-STARCHY VEGETABLES: Brussels sprouts, radishes, cabbage, bell pepper
- FRUITS: Avocado
- WHOLE FOOD FATS: Bacon, avocado, nuts, olive oil
- HIGH-QUALITY PROTEINS: Bacon
- FLAVOR ENHANCERS: Parsley, red pepper flakes, dressing

Shrimp & Portobello Mushroom Salad

Packed with juicy shrimp, tender sautéed mushrooms, fresh spinach, and creamy avocado, this salad is a vibrant mix of bright, earthy flavors and rich textures that hits all the right notes!

YIELD: 4 servings • **PREP TIME:** 15 minutes • **COOK TIME:** 10 minutes • **TOTAL TIME:** 25 minutes

FOR THE SHRIMP:
1 tablespoon (15 ml) fresh lime juice
2 tablespoons (30 ml) extra-virgin olive oil, divided
2 garlic cloves, minced
½ teaspoon smoked paprika
Salt and pepper, to taste
1 pound (450 g) shrimp, peeled and deveined

FOR THE AVOCADO CILANTRO LIME DRESSING:
1 avocado, peeled and pitted
2 tablespoons (30 ml) extra-virgin olive oil
¼ cup (60 ml) fresh lime juice
¼ cup (4 g) fresh cilantro, chopped
1 tablespoon (15 ml) apple cider vinegar
1 teaspoon Dijon mustard
1 or 2 cloves garlic, minced
½ teaspoon ground cumin
3 to 4 tablespoons (45 to 60 ml) water, as needed
Salt and pepper, to taste

FOR THE BOWL:
1 tablespoon (15 ml) extra-virgin olive oil, divided
4 large portobello mushrooms, stems removed and sliced
6 to 8 cups (180 to 240 g) baby spinach
½ small red onion, thinly sliced
1 avocado, peeled, pitted, and sliced
¼ cup (38 g) crumbled feta cheese
2 tablespoons (5 g) fresh basil, finely chopped (optional)

PREPARE THE SHRIMP: In a medium bowl, whisk together the lime juice, 1 tablespoon (15 ml) olive oil, garlic, paprika, salt, and pepper. Add the shrimp and toss to coat well. Let sit for 10 to 15 minutes. Using the same skillet, heat the remaining olive oil over medium-high heat. Add the marinated shrimp and cook for 2 to 3 minutes per side until pink and fully cooked through. Remove from the heat.

MAKE THE DRESSING: Add all the dressing ingredients to a blender or food processor. Start on low speed and gradually increase the speed until smooth. Add water as needed for desired consistency. Adjust the seasoning to taste.

SAUTÉ THE MUSHROOMS: Heat the olive oil in a large skillet over medium-high heat. Add the mushrooms and cook for 5 to 6 minutes, stirring occasionally, until tender and slightly browned. Remove from the skillet.

BUILD THE BOWL: In a large bowl, toss the spinach and onion with a drizzle of dressing. Divide the salad among four bowls and top with mushrooms, avocado, shrimp, and feta. Drizzle the remaining dressing over each bowl and sprinkle with basil (if using). Serve immediately.

NOTES

CUSTOMIZE YOUR PROTEIN: Swap the shrimp with chicken, salmon, or tofu for a flexible, nutrient-packed salad. Each protein pairs well with the zesty dressing and complements the salad's fresh flavors.

NUTRITIONAL ANALYSIS

PER SERVING: 460 calories; 35 g fat; 15 g carbohydrates; 7 g dietary fiber; 4 g sugars; 29 g protein

The Build Your Bowl System Profile

- **NON-STARCHY VEGETABLES:** Spinach, mushrooms, onion
- **FRUITS:** Avocado
- **WHOLE FOOD FATS:** Avocado, cheese, olive oil
- **HIGH-QUALITY PROTEINS:** Shrimp, cheese
- **FLAVOR ENHANCERS:** Cheese, basil, marinade, dressing

Grilled Chicken & Zucchini Noodles Bowl

A great low-carb alternative to traditional pasta, this bowl delivers vibrant flavors, satisfying textures, and a balanced mix of nutrients for overall well-being.

YIELD: 4 servings • **PREP TIME:** 15 minutes plus 10 minutes to marinate • **COOK TIME:** 20 minutes • **TOTAL TIME:** 45 minutes

FOR THE CHICKEN:

1 tablespoon (15 ml) extra-virgin olive oil
1 teaspoon garlic powder
1 teaspoon onion powder
½ teaspoon smoked paprika
Salt and pepper, to taste
3 medium boneless, skinless chicken breasts (about 1 pound, or 450 g, total)

FOR THE ZESTY LEMON GARLIC DRESSING:

¼ cup (60 ml) extra-virgin olive oil
2 tablespoons (30 ml) fresh lemon juice
1 clove garlic, minced
1 teaspoon Dijon mustard
½ teaspoon honey or a low-carb sweetener, optional
½ teaspoon dried thyme
Salt and pepper, to taste

FOR THE BOWL:

1 tablespoon (15 ml) extra-virgin olive oil
2 cloves garlic, minced
½ cup (50 g) cremini or button mushrooms, sliced
1 yellow bell pepper, cored and thinly sliced
3 large zucchinis, spiralized into noodles
Salt and pepper, to taste
1 tablespoon (1 g) fresh cilantro, chopped
1 tablespoon (6 g) fresh mint, chopped
1 large beefsteak tomato, diced
½ cucumber, thinly sliced
1 avocado, peeled, pitted, and sliced

PREPARE THE CHICKEN: Combine the seasonings in a small bowl and rub the mixture onto the chicken breasts. Let marinate for at least 10 minutes. Preheat a grill or grill pan to medium-high heat. Grill the chicken for 6 to 8 minutes per side, or until the internal temperature reaches 165°F (74°C). Let rest for 5 minutes before slicing into strips.

MAKE THE DRESSING: In a small bowl, shaker, or mason jar, combine all the dressing ingredients. Whisk or shake until well mixed. Adjust the seasoning to taste.

PREPARE THE ZUCCHINI NOODLES: Heat the olive oil in a large skillet over medium heat. Add the garlic and sauté for about 1 minute until fragrant. Add the mushrooms and bell pepper, cooking for 3 to 4 minutes until tender. Add the zucchini noodles and cook for another 2 minutes until just tender. Season with salt and pepper, then toss with cilantro and mint.

BUILD THE BOWL: Divide the zucchini noodles and sautéed vegetables among four bowls. Top with chicken, tomato, cucumber, and avocado. Drizzle with the dressing and serve immediately.

NOTES

FLAVOR ENHANCERS: For a spicier version, add red pepper flakes to the vegetables while they sauté or mix them into the dressing for a subtle kick.

NUTRITIONAL ANALYSIS

PER SERVING: 445 calories; 30 g fat; 18 g carbohydrates; 6 g dietary fiber; 7 g sugars; 30 g protein

The Build Your Bowl System Profile

- **NON-STARCHY VEGETABLES:** Zucchini, bell pepper, mushrooms, tomato, cucumber
- **FRUITS:** Avocado
- **WHOLE FOOD FATS:** Olive oil, avocado
- **HIGH-QUALITY PROTEINS:** Chicken
- **FLAVOR ENHANCERS:** Herbs, seasonings, dressing

Italian Chopped Salad with Sausage

Combining layers of bold flavors and textures, this easy-to-customize Italian chopped salad features savory sausage, crisp greens, and vibrant veggies, all topped with crunchy pine nuts and a zesty vinaigrette.

YIELD: 4 servings • **PREP TIME:** 15 minutes • **COOK TIME:** 15 minutes • **TOTAL TIME:** 30 minutes

FOR THE ITALIAN VINAIGRETTE:

3 tablespoons (45 ml) extra-virgin olive oil
2 tablespoons (30 ml) white wine vinegar
1 tablespoon (15 ml) fresh lemon juice
1 teaspoon Dijon mustard
1 teaspoon dried oregano
1 clove garlic, minced
¼ teaspoon red pepper flakes (optional)
Salt and pepper, to taste

FOR THE BOWL:

1 tablespoon (15 ml) extra-virgin olive oil
1 pound (450 g) ground Italian sausage (pork, chicken, or turkey)
4 cups (200 g) chopped romaine lettuce
2 cups (80 g) chopped radicchio
2 cups (40 g) arugula, chopped
Salt and pepper, to taste
1 yellow bell pepper, diced
1 large Roma tomato, seeded and diced
1 small cucumber, diced
1 small red onion, thinly sliced
¼ cup (33 g) Kalamata olives, pitted and sliced
¼ cup (25 g) grated Parmesan cheese, or more to taste
¼ cup (35 g) toasted pine nuts (optional)
2 tablespoons (5 g) fresh basil, chopped

MAKE THE DRESSING: Add all the dressing ingredients to a small bowl, shaker, or mason jar. Whisk or shake until well mixed. Adjust the seasoning to taste.

COOK THE SAUSAGE: Heat the olive oil in a skillet over medium heat. Add the Italian sausage, breaking it up with a spatula. Cook until browned and fully done, 7 to 10 minutes. Remove from the heat.

BUILD THE BOWL: In a large bowl, combine the romaine lettuce, radicchio, and arugula. Season with salt and pepper, then drizzle with dressing and gently toss to coat well. Add the bell pepper, tomato, cucumber, onion, olives, Parmesan, and pine nuts and toss again. Divide the salad among four bowls, top with cooked sausage, and garnish with fresh basil. Serve immediately.

NOTES

CHOOSING SAUSAGE: When selecting sausage, look for options with minimal fillers and added sugars. You can also swap the Italian sausage with grilled chicken, turkey, or plant-based sausage for a different twist.

FLAVOR ENHANCERS: Fresh herbs like parsley or thyme can boost the bowl's flavors even more.

NUTRITIONAL ANALYSIS

PER SERVING: 529 calories; 44 g fat; 15 g carbohydrates; 4 g dietary fiber; 4 g sugars; 21 g protein

The Build Your Bowl System Profile

- NON-STARCHY VEGETABLES: Lettuce, radicchio, arugula, bell pepper, tomato, cucumber, onion
- WHOLE FOOD FATS: Olive oil, olives, cheese, pine nuts
- HIGH-QUALITY PROTEINS: Sausage (see notes), cheese
- FLAVOR ENHANCERS: Basil, dressing

Lemon Herb Mahi-mahi Bowl

This fresh, flavorful bowl combines flaky mahi-mahi with crisp greens, creamy avocado, tangy feta, and a zesty lemon dill vinaigrette for a bright, satisfying finish.

YIELD: 4 servings • **PREP TIME:** 20 minutes plus 15 minutes to marinate • **COOK TIME:** 15 minutes • **TOTAL TIME:** 50 minutes

FOR THE MAHI-MAHI:

3 tablespoons (45 ml) fresh lemon juice
1 tablespoon (15 ml) extra-virgin olive oil
1 tablespoon (15 g) fresh Italian parsley, chopped
1 teaspoon garlic powder
1 teaspoon smoked paprika or ground cumin
Salt and pepper, to taste
4 mahi-mahi fillets (about 1 pound, or 450 g, total)

FOR THE LEMON DILL VINAIGRETTE:

¼ cup (60 ml) extra-virgin olive oil
2 tablespoons (30 ml) fresh lemon juice
1 tablespoon (15 ml) white wine vinegar
1 tablespoon (11 g) Dijon mustard
1 tablespoon (4 g) fresh dill, chopped
1 teaspoon pure honey (optional)
1 clove garlic, minced
Salt and pepper, to taste

FOR THE BOWL:

8 cups (440 g) mixed greens
2 Roma tomatoes, seeded and diced
1 small cucumber, diced
½ medium red onion, thinly sliced
¼ cup (33 g) Kalamata olives, pitted and sliced
1 avocado, peeled, pitted, and sliced or diced
¼ cup (38 g) crumbled feta cheese (optional)
¼ cup (35 g) toasted pine nuts or slivered almonds (optional)

PREPARE THE MAHI-MAHI: In a small bowl, whisk together all the marinade ingredients. Place the fillets in a shallow dish, pour the marinade over them, and coat evenly. Cover and marinate in the fridge for 15 to 30 minutes. Preheat the oven to 400°F (200°C). Transfer the marinated fillets to a parchment-lined baking sheet, pouring any remaining marinade over the top. Bake for 12 to 15 minutes, or until the fish is cooked through and flakes easily with a fork. Remove from the oven and let rest for a few minutes before serving.

MAKE THE DRESSING: In a small bowl, shaker, or mason jar, combine all the dressing ingredients. Whisk or shake until well mixed. Adjust the seasoning to taste.

BUILD THE BOWL: Place the mixed greens in a large bowl, drizzle with the dressing, and toss to coat. Add the tomatoes, cucumber, onion, and olives, tossing with more dressing to taste. Divide the salad among four bowls. Top each with a fillet and some avocado, then finish with feta and pine nuts (if using). Serve immediately with extra dressing on the side.

NOTES

MAKE IT YOUR OWN: Swap mahi-mahi with salmon or shrimp, and customize with roasted veggies, quinoa, or nuts and seeds for extra texture and variety.

NUTRITIONAL ANALYSIS

PER SERVING: 440 calories; 31 g fat; 17 g carbohydrates; 6 g dietary fiber; 6 g sugars; 27 g protein

The Build Your Bowl System Profile

- **NON-STARCHY VEGETABLES:** Mixed greens, tomatoes, cucumber, onion
- **WHOLE FOOD FATS:** Olives, avocado, olive oil, cheese, nuts
- **HIGH-QUALITY PROTEINS:** Mahi-mahi, cheese
- **FLAVOR ENHANCERS:** Cheese, marinade, dressing

Creamy Chicken & Avocado Salad

This keto bowl strikes the perfect balance of creamy and crunchy, combining tender chicken with fresh, crisp veggies, all brought together by a rich herb vinaigrette.

YIELD: 4 servings • **PREP TIME:** 20 minutes • **COOK TIME:** 15 minutes • **TOTAL TIME:** 35 minutes

FOR THE CHICKEN:

2 medium boneless, skinless chicken breasts (about 14 ounces, or 400 g, total)
Salt and pepper, to taste
1 tablespoon (weight varies) your favorite dried herbs

FOR THE CREAMY HERB VINAIGRETTE:

⅓ cup (80 g) mayonnaise (ideally avocado oil-based)
¼ cup (60 g) sour cream
2 to 3 tablespoons (30 to 45 ml) white wine vinegar
1 tablespoon (4 g) fresh dill, finely chopped
1 tablespoon (10 g) finely chopped fresh chives
1 teaspoon Dijon mustard
1 clove garlic, minced
1 to 2 tablespoons (15 to 30 ml) water, as needed
Salt and pepper, to taste

FOR THE BOWL:

6 to 8 cups (300 to 400 g) chopped romaine lettuce
½ small red cabbage, thinly sliced
1 medium cucumber, diced
¼ red onion, thinly sliced
4 or 5 radishes, thinly sliced
2 large avocados, peeled, pitted, and diced
¼ cup (40 g) toasted pepitas
¼ cup (4 g) fresh cilantro, chopped (optional)

PREPARE THE CHICKEN: Season the chicken breasts with salt, pepper, and your favorite dried herbs. Heat a lightly greased skillet or grill-pan over medium heat. Add the chicken and cook for 6 to 7 minutes per side until the internal temperature reaches 165°F (74°C). Remove from the heat and let rest for 5 minutes, then shred or dice.

MAKE THE DRESSING: Combine all the dressing ingredients in a blender or food processor. Start at a low speed and gradually increase the speed until the mixture is smooth and well combined. Add water as needed to reach your desired consistency. Season with salt and pepper to taste. Alternatively, whisk the dressing ingredients in a small bowl until well blended.

BUILD THE BOWL: In a large bowl, toss the romaine and cabbage with some of the dressing until evenly coated. Add the cucumber, onion, and radishes, tossing with additional dressing to taste. Gently fold in the chicken and avocados. Divide the salad evenly among four bowls. Top each with pepitas and garnish with cilantro, if desired. Drizzle with more dressing, if needed, and serve.

NOTES

DRESSING ALTERNATIVES: For a lighter option, replace sour cream with Greek yogurt if not following a strict keto diet. For a dairy-free alternative, use unsweetened plain coconut yogurt instead of sour cream.

FLAVOR ENHANCERS: Sprinkle with a dash of smoked paprika or red pepper flakes for added spice.

NUTRITIONAL ANALYSIS

PER SERVING: 420 calories; 27 g fat; 19 g carbohydrates; 9 g dietary fiber; 5 g sugars; 29 g protein

The Build Your Bowl System Profile

- NON-STARCHY VEGETABLES: Lettuce, cabbage, cucumber, onion, radishes
- FRUITS: Avocado
- WHOLE FOOD FATS: Avocado, mayonnaise, sour cream, pepitas
- HIGH-QUALITY PROTEINS: Chicken
- FLAVOR ENHANCERS: Cilantro, dressing

Spiced Cauliflower & Crispy Tofu Almond Bowl

Packed with plant-based protein, healthy fats, and bold flavors, this keto-friendly bowl combines roasted cauliflower, tofu, and mixed greens with a refreshing lime vinaigrette.

YIELD: 4 servings • **PREP TIME:** 20 minutes plus 20 minutes to marinate • **COOK TIME:** 25 minutes • **TOTAL TIME:** 1 hour 5 minutes

FOR THE ZESTY LIME VINAIGRETTE:

5 tablespoons (75 ml) extra-virgin olive oil
3 tablespoons (45 ml) fresh lime juice
1 teaspoon apple cider vinegar
½ teaspoon Dijon mustard
½ teaspoon monk fruit sweetener or liquid stevia (optional)
1 clove garlic, minced
Salt and pepper, to taste

FOR THE CAULIFLOWER AND TOFU:

1 medium head cauliflower, cut into bite-size florets
1 small block (7 ounces, or 200 g) organic extra-firm tofu, drained
1 teaspoon smoked paprika
¾ teaspoon ground cumin
¾ teaspoon garlic powder
½ teaspoon onion powder
¼ teaspoon cayenne pepper (optional)

FOR THE BOWL:

6 cups (330 g) mixed greens
Salt and pepper, to taste
½ small red onion, thinly sliced
1 small cucumber, diced
½ red bell pepper, thinly sliced
1 avocado, peeled, pitted, and sliced
¼ cup (30 g) toasted almonds, chopped
1 tablespoon (8 g) sesame seeds (optional)
¼ cup (4 g) fresh cilantro, chopped (optional)

MAKE THE DRESSING: Whisk all the dressing ingredients in a bowl until well combined. Reserve half for the salad and use the rest as a marinade.

PREPARE THE CAULIFLOWER AND TOFU: Press the tofu for 15 to 20 minutes using a tofu press or by placing it between a towel and a heavy object. Crumble into bite-size pieces. In a large bowl, toss the tofu and cauliflower with the seasonings. Pour in half the dressing and toss gently to coat. Marinate for 20 minutes to 1 hour. Preheat the oven to 400°F (200°C). Spread the cauliflower mixture on a parchment-lined baking sheet. Roast for 20 to 25 minutes, stirring halfway, until the cauliflower is tender and charred, and the tofu is golden and crisp.

BUILD THE BOWL: Arrange the mixed greens in a large bowl. Season with salt and pepper, drizzle with dressing, and toss gently. Add the onion, cucumber, and bell pepper, drizzling with more dressing if desired. Divide the salad among four bowls. Top each with roasted cauliflower and tofu, avocado, almonds, and sesame seeds (if using). Drizzle with additional dressing, garnish with cilantro (if using), and serve immediately.

NOTES

ENHANCE THE FLAVOR: Toss in a few pickled onions, jalapeños, or pepperoncini to add tang and contrast.

NUTRITIONAL ANALYSIS

PER SERVING: 400 calories; 32 g fat; 24 g carbohydrates; 10 g dietary fiber; 6 g sugars; 14 g protein

The Build Your Bowl System Profile

- **NON-STARCHY VEGETABLES:** Cauliflower, mixed greens, onion, cucumber, bell pepper
- **FRUITS:** Avocado
- **WHOLE FOOD FATS:** Avocado, almonds, sesame seeds, olive oil
- **HIGH-QUALITY PROTEINS:** Tofu
- **FLAVOR ENHANCERS:** Cilantro, sesame seeds, seasonings, dressing

Eggplant Parmesan Spinach Salad

A nutritious twist on a classic comfort food, this keto-friendly bowl swaps traditional breading and pasta for tender eggplant, fresh spinach, and vibrant veggies.

YIELD: 4 servings • **PREP TIME:** 20 minutes • **COOK TIME:** 25 minutes • **TOTAL TIME:** 45 minutes

FOR THE EGGPLANT:
1 large eggplant, sliced into ¼-inch (6 mm) rounds
2 tablespoons (30 ml) extra-virgin olive oil
¼ teaspoon salt
⅛ teaspoon pepper
¼ cup (30 g) almond flour
¼ cup (30 g) grated Parmesan cheese

FOR THE LEMON BASIL VINAIGRETTE:
¼ cup (60 ml) extra-virgin olive oil
2 tablespoons (30 ml) fresh lemon juice
2 tablespoons (30 ml) red wine vinegar
1 clove garlic, minced
1 tablespoon (11 g) Dijon mustard
¼ cup (10 g) fresh basil, finely chopped
Salt and pepper, to taste

FOR THE BOWL:
8 cups (240 g) baby spinach
1 cup (150 g) cherry tomatoes, halved
½ cup (60 g) roasted red peppers, sliced
¼ cup (30 g) fresh mozzarella, torn into pieces (optional)
¼ cup (30 g) sliced toasted almonds

PREPARE THE EGGPLANT: Preheat the oven to 400°F (200°C). Line a baking sheet with parchment paper. Arrange the eggplant on the sheet, brush with the olive oil, and season with the salt and pepper. Mix the almond flour and Parmesan in a small bowl, then sprinkle evenly over the eggplant. Bake for 20 to 25 minutes until tender and golden brown. Let cool slightly.

MAKE THE DRESSING: In a small bowl, shaker, or mason jar, combine all the dressing ingredients. Whisk or shake until well mixed. Adjust the seasoning to taste.

BUILD THE BOWL: In a large bowl, combine the spinach, tomatoes, peppers, and mozzarella (if using). Drizzle with half the dressing and toss to coat evenly. Divide the salad among four bowls. Top each with a few slices of baked eggplant. Sprinkle with almonds and drizzle with the remaining dressing. Serve immediately.

NOTES

CUSTOMIZE YOUR PROTEIN: Boost the protein by adding grilled chicken, shrimp, or Italian sausage.

FLAVOR ENHANCERS: Fresh herbs like parsley or thyme can add additional flavor to this dish.

NUTRITIONAL ANALYSIS

PER SERVING: 355 calories; 27 g fat; 17 g carbohydrates; 8 g dietary fiber; 8 g sugars; 10 g protein

The Build Your Bowl System Profile

- NON-STARCHY VEGETABLES: Eggplant, spinach, tomatoes, peppers
- WHOLE FOOD FATS: Olive oil, almond flour, almonds, cheese
- HIGH-QUALITY PROTEINS: Cheese
- FLAVOR ENHANCERS: Basil, dressing

Spaghetti Squash & Meatball Bowl

A unique twist on a classic comfort meal, this low-carb bowl combines roasted spaghetti squash with juicy meatballs and a colorful mix of fresh vegetables for a flavorful and satisfying lunch or dinner.

YIELD: 4 servings • **PREP TIME:** 20 minutes • **COOK TIME:** 40 minutes • **TOTAL TIME:** 1 hour

FOR THE SQUASH:

1 large spaghetti squash
1 tablespoon (15 ml) extra-virgin olive oil
Salt and pepper, to taste

FOR THE MEATBALLS:

1 pound (450 g) ground beef (93% lean)
⅓ cup (33 g) grated Parmesan cheese
1 large egg
2 cloves garlic, minced
1 tablespoon (15 g) tomato paste
1 teaspoon dried oregano
1 teaspoon dried basil
½ teaspoon onion powder
Salt and pepper, to taste
1 tablespoon (15 ml) extra-virgin olive oil

FOR THE GARLIC PARMESAN DRESSING:

3 tablespoons (45 ml) extra-virgin olive oil
2 tablespoons (30 ml) fresh lemon juice
2 cloves garlic, minced
2 tablespoons (15 g) grated Parmesan cheese
1 teaspoon Dijon mustard
½ teaspoon dried thyme
Salt and pepper, to taste

FOR THE BOWL:

6 to 8 cups (180 to 240 g) baby spinach
1 bell pepper (red or yellow), cored and thinly sliced
1 cup (150 g) cherry tomatoes, halved
½ cup (75 g) black olives, pitted and sliced
½ cucumber, thinly sliced
2 tablespoons (8 g) fresh Italian parsley, chopped
Salt and pepper, to taste

ROAST THE SQUASH: Preheat the oven to 400°F (200°C). Halve the squash lengthwise, scoop out the seeds, and drizzle with the olive oil. Season with salt and pepper. Place the squash halves, cut-side down, on a baking sheet and roast for 30 to 40 minutes until the flesh is tender. Let cool, then scrape the flesh into strands with a fork.

PREPARE THE MEATBALLS: In a large bowl, mix the beef and seasonings. Form 12 meatballs by hand. Heat the olive oil in a skillet over medium heat and cook the meatballs for 8 to 10 minutes, turning until browned and cooked through. Set aside.

MAKE THE DRESSING: In a small bowl, shaker, or mason jar, combine all the dressing ingredients. Whisk or shake until well mixed. Adjust the seasoning to taste.

BUILD THE BOWL: In a large bowl, toss the spinach, bell pepper, tomatoes, olives, cucumber, and parsley with salt, pepper, and a drizzle of dressing. Divide among four bowls, top each with squash, three meatballs, and more dressing. Garnish with parsley, if desired. Serve immediately.

NOTES

SERVE IT WARM: Sauté the bell pepper, tomatoes, and olives in olive oil until softened, and omit the spinach to enjoy a warm, satisfying dish.

NUTRITIONAL ANALYSIS

PER SERVING: 535 calories; 33 g fat; 31 g carbohydrates; 8 g dietary fiber; 12 g sugars; 33 g protein

The Build Your Bowl System Profile

- NON-STARCHY VEGETABLES: Spinach, spaghetti squash, bell pepper, tomatoes, cucumber
- FRUITS: Olives
- WHOLE FOOD FATS: Olive oil, cheese
- HIGH-QUALITY PROTEINS: Ground beef, cheese
- FLAVOR ENHANCERS: Parsley, cheese, seasonings, dressing

Seared Pork Tenderloin & Kale Salad

Combining the rich flavors of seared pork tenderloin, tender massaged kale, and a tangy red wine vinaigrette, this low-carb bowl is as hearty as it gets.

YIELD: 4 servings • **PREP TIME:** 15 minutes plus 30 minutes to marinate • **COOK TIME:** 25 minutes • **TOTAL TIME:** 1 hour 10 minutes

FOR THE PORK TENDERLOIN:

1 pound (450 g) pork tenderloin, trimmed
1 teaspoon smoked paprika
½ teaspoon garlic powder
½ teaspoon onion powder
½ teaspoon dried thyme
Salt and pepper, to taste
1 tablespoon (15 ml) extra-virgin olive oil

FOR THE RED WINE VINAIGRETTE:

¼ cup (60 ml) extra-virgin olive oil
2 to 3 tablespoons (30 to 45 ml) red wine vinegar
2 teaspoons Dijon mustard
2 teaspoons fresh lemon juice
1 clove garlic, minced
Salt and pepper, to taste

FOR THE BOWL:

6 to 8 cups (400 to 535 g) finely chopped stemmed kale
¼ small red onion, thinly sliced
½ small orange bell pepper, thinly sliced
4 or 5 radishes, thinly sliced
1 avocado, peeled, pitted, and sliced
¼ cup (40 g) toasted pepitas
¼ cup (30 g) grated Parmesan cheese (optional)

PREPARE THE PORK TENDERLOIN: Preheat the oven to 400°F (200°C). Coat the pork tenderloin with the seasonings and marinate in the fridge for at least 30 minutes. Heat the olive oil in a skillet over medium-high heat. Sear the tenderloin on all sides for 2 to 3 minutes per side until browned. Transfer to a baking sheet and roast in the oven for 15 to 20 minutes, or until the internal temperature reaches 145°F (63°C). *Do not* exceed this temperature or the pork won't be juicy and tender. Let rest for 5 minutes, then slice into medallions.

MAKE THE DRESSING: In a small bowl, shaker, or mason jar, combine all the dressing ingredients. Whisk or shake until well mixed. Adjust the seasoning to taste.

BUILD THE BOWL: Place the kale in a large bowl and drizzle with half the dressing. Massage the leaves for 1 to 2 minutes to soften them. Add the onion, bell pepper, and radishes and toss gently to combine. Divide the kale mixture evenly among four bowls. Top each with avocado, pepitas, and Parmesan (if using). Add the pork tenderloin and drizzle with additional dressing to taste. Serve immediately.

NOTES

CUSTOMIZE YOUR PROTEIN: Swap the pork tenderloin with grilled chicken or sirloin.

FLAVOR ENHANCERS: For a slightly sweeter dressing, add a dash of monk fruit sweetener or a few drops of stevia. You can also add a pinch of red pepper flakes for a spicy kick.

NUTRITIONAL ANALYSIS

PER SERVING: 430 calories; 31 g fat; 10 g carbohydrates; 5 g dietary fiber; 2 g sugars; 30 g protein

The Build Your Bowl System Profile

- NON-STARCHY VEGETABLES: Kale, onion, bell pepper, radishes
- FRUITS: Avocado
- WHOLE FOOD FATS: Avocado, pepitas, cheese, olive oil
- HIGH-QUALITY PROTEINS: Pork tenderloin, cheese
- FLAVOR ENHANCERS: Seasonings, dressing

Korean Beef Salad with Lettuce Wraps

This vibrant salad brings a fresh spin to Korean-inspired cuisine with perfectly marinated beef, crisp veggies, and a creamy miso lime dressing. Enjoy as a salad or in a lettuce wrap!

YIELD: 4 servings • **PREP TIME:** 20 minutes plus 30 minutes to marinate • **COOK TIME:** 15 minutes • **TOTAL TIME:** 1 hour 5 minutes

FOR THE BEEF:

2 tablespoons (30 ml) low-sodium tamari
1 tablespoon (15 ml) toasted sesame oil, plus 1½ teaspoons
1 tablespoon (15 ml) rice vinegar
1 tablespoon (15 ml) fresh lime juice
1 clove garlic, minced
1 teaspoon minced fresh ginger
1 teaspoon sriracha (optional)
1 pound (450 g) beef sirloin or flank steak, thinly sliced

FOR THE CREAMY MISO LIME DRESSING:

2 tablespoons (30 ml) toasted sesame oil
2 tablespoons (30 g) white miso paste
1 tablespoon (15 ml) rice vinegar
2 tablespoons (30 ml) fresh lime juice
1 tablespoon (15 g) tahini (optional)
1 teaspoon minced fresh ginger
1 clove garlic, minced
½ teaspoon monk fruit sweetener or liquid stevia
2 to 3 tablespoons (30 to 45 ml) water, as needed

FOR THE BOWL:

2 medium heads baby bok choy, shredded
½ small red cabbage, shredded
½ small daikon radish, spiralized or julienned
½ medium cucumber, thinly sliced
1 small carrot, julienned
Salt and pepper, to taste
½ avocado, peeled, pitted, and sliced
2 scallions, thinly sliced
2 tablespoons (30 g) toasted sesame seeds
1 head butter lettuce, leaves separated (optional)

PREPARE THE BEEF: Mix the tamari, 1 tablespoon (15 ml) of the sesame oil, vinegar, lime juice, garlic, ginger, and sriracha (if using) in a medium bowl. Add the beef and toss to coat. Cover and refrigerate for 30 minutes to 2 hours. Heat the remaining 1½ teaspoons sesame oil in a large skillet over medium-high heat. Stir-fry the marinated beef for 4 to 5 minutes until browned and cooked through. Set aside and let cool slightly.

MAKE THE DRESSING: Combine all the dressing ingredients in a small bowl and whisk until smooth. Add water as needed.

BUILD THE BOWL: In a large bowl, combine the bok choy, cabbage, radish, cucumber, and carrot with salt, pepper and a drizzle of dressing. Toss until everything is evenly coated.

SERVE: Divide the salad among four bowls, top with the beef, drizzle with the dressing, and garnish with avocado, scallions, and sesame seeds. Enjoy as a salad or use the butter lettuce leaves as wraps.

NOTES

CUSTOMIZE YOUR BOWL: Stir-fry veggies for warmth or add low-carb options like zucchini or bell peppers. Swap beef with pork, chicken, or tofu for a plant-based twist.

NUTRITIONAL ANALYSIS

PER SERVING: 425 calories; 27 g fat; 18 g carbohydrates; 5 g dietary fiber; 6 g sugars; 31 g protein

The Build Your Bowl System Profile

- NON-STARCHY VEGETABLES: Bok choy, lettuce, cabbage, radish, cucumber, carrot
- WHOLE FOOD FATS: Avocado, sesame oil
- HIGH-QUALITY PROTEINS: Beef
- FLAVOR ENHANCERS: Scallions, sesame seeds, marinade, dressing

7

Nourishing Heart-Healthy Bowls

I simply couldn't put together a collection of recipes without highlighting heart-healthy bowls. The heart is at the center of our overall well-being—when it functions well, the rest of the body tends to follow. That's why this chapter is dedicated to bowls that support a healthy heart without sacrificing flavor.

Maintaining heart health comes down to balancing quality fats, lean proteins, and a variety of colorful vegetables. For instance, the Seared Salmon and Mixed Berry Salad (page 141) combines wild salmon with a trio of fresh berries and a tangy raspberry vinaigrette, delivering a tasty mix of flavors and heart-protective nutrients.

Bringing Mediterranean vibes, the Classic Greek Salad with Toasted Quinoa (page 130) features crunchy vegetables, creamy avocado, and nutrient-dense quinoa in a light yet satisfying dish. For a bolder option, the Chicken and Roasted Beet Kale Salad (page 138) pairs lean protein, roasted beets, and a creamy tahini dressing that ties the flavors together beautifully.

And don't forget the Kale Caesar Salad with Crispy Chickpeas (page 148), a nutritious twist on the classic, or the Mediterranean Tuna and White Bean Salad (page 134) with protein-rich tuna, fiber-packed beans, and a zesty lemon oregano vinaigrette.

With these recipes and more, you can support your heart with meals you'll genuinely enjoy. Plus, many heart-healthy ingredients also protect against chronic conditions like diabetes and certain cancers, making these bowls great for your overall well-being.

Classic Greek Salad with Toasted Quinoa

Mediterranean-style diets are celebrated for supporting heart health. This Greek salad offers a wholesome twist on a classic, combining simplicity, rich flavors, and nutritious ingredients for a light yet satisfying meal.

YIELD: 4 servings • **PREP TIME:** 20 minutes • **COOK TIME:** 15 minutes • **TOTAL TIME:** 35 minutes

FOR THE RED WINE VINAIGRETTE:

⅓ cup (80 ml) extra-virgin olive oil
¼ cup (60 ml) red wine vinegar
1 tablespoon (11 g) Dijon mustard
2 teaspoons dried oregano
2 cloves garlic, minced
Salt and pepper, to taste

FOR THE BOWL:

1 cup (170 g) quinoa (tricolored if available)
2 cups (480 ml) water or low-sodium vegetable broth
8 cups (440 g) mixed greens
2 bell peppers (orange and yellow), diced
1 cucumber, seeded and diced
½ red onion, diced
2 cups (300 g) grape tomatoes, halved
½ cup (65 g) Kalamata olives, pitted and sliced
1 avocado, peeled, pitted, and diced
¼ cup (38 g) crumbled feta cheese (optional)

MAKE THE DRESSING: In a small bowl, whisk all the dressing ingredients together until well combined.

TOAST THE QUINOA: Rinse and drain the quinoa thoroughly. Add it to a medium saucepan and toast over medium heat, stirring frequently, for 3 to 4 minutes until fragrant and slightly golden. Add the water, bring to a boil, then reduce the heat and simmer, covered, for 12 to 15 minutes until the liquid is absorbed. Fluff with a fork and let cool.

BUILD THE BOWL: Toss the mixed greens with dressing in a large bowl. Add the bell peppers, cucumber, onion, tomatoes, and olives and toss gently to combine. Mix in the quinoa and avocado, adding more dressing if needed. Divide among four bowls and top with feta, if using. Serve immediately.

NOTES

LOWER THE CALORIES: This salad is rich in health-promoting fats, which contribute to the calorie count. If you're mindful of calories, adjust the portions by reducing the dressing, olives, and cheese, or using a smaller amount of quinoa.

BOOST THE PROTEIN: Add grilled chicken or tofu for an extra protein boost, making the salad even more satisfying.

FLAVOR ENHANCERS: Fresh herbs like basil, parsley, or dill can enhance the flavor and add a burst of freshness to the salad.

NUTRITIONAL ANALYSIS

PER SERVING: 484 calories; 30 g fat; 45 g carbohydrates; 10 g dietary fiber; 7 g sugars; 11 g protein

The Build Your Bowl System Profile

- **NON-STARCHY VEGETABLES:** Mixed greens, bell peppers, cucumber, onion, tomatoes
- **FRUITS:** Avocado
- **WHOLE FOOD FATS:** Avocado, olives, cheese, olive oil
- **HIGH-QUALITY PROTEINS:** Quinoa, cheese
- **FIBER-RICH STARCHES:** Quinoa
- **FLAVOR ENHANCERS:** Cheese, dressing

Citrus Salmon & Avocado Lentil Salad

The trio of salmon, avocado, and lentils in this heart-healthy bowl offers hefty doses of quality fats, protein, and fiber while citrus fruits brighten the dish and boosts iron absorption from the spinach and lentils.

YIELD: 4 servings • **PREP TIME:** 15 minutes • **COOK TIME:** 25 minutes • **TOTAL TIME:** 40 minutes

FOR THE LENTILS:

½ cup (100 g) lentils (black, green, or brown)
1½ cups (360 ml) water or low-sodium vegetable broth

FOR THE SALMON:

4 wild-caught, skinless salmon fillets (about 4 ounces, or 115 g, each)
Salt and pepper, to taste
1 teaspoon garlic powder

FOR THE CITRUS VINAIGRETTE:

¼ cup (60 ml) extra-virgin olive oil
3 tablespoons (45 ml) fresh orange juice
1 tablespoon (15 ml) fresh lemon juice
1 tablespoon (20 g) pure honey
1 teaspoon Dijon mustard
1 clove garlic, minced
Salt and pepper, to taste

FOR THE BOWL:

8 cups (240 g) baby spinach
1 avocado, peeled, pitted, and sliced
1 orange, peeled and segmented
1 grapefruit, peeled and segmented
½ medium red onion, thinly sliced

COOK THE LENTILS: Rinse the lentils under cold water. Add to a medium saucepan with the water. Bring to a boil over medium heat, then reduce the heat, cover, and simmer for 20 to 25 minutes, or until tender. Drain any excess liquid and set the lentils aside to cool.

BAKE THE SALMON: Preheat the oven to 375°F (190°C). Season the fillets with salt, pepper, and garlic powder. Place on a baking sheet lined with parchment paper and bake for 12 to 15 minutes, or until the salmon is cooked through and flakes easily with a fork. Allow to cool slightly, then break into large chunks.

MAKE THE DRESSING: Add all the dressing ingredients to a small bowl, shaker, or mason jar. Whisk or shake until well mixed.

BUILD THE BOWL: Lay out the spinach in a large bowl, drizzle with the dressing, and mix well. Arrange the avocado, orange, grapefruit, and onion over the dressed greens. Add the salmon and lentils, then drizzle with more dressing if desired. Gently toss everything together and serve immediately.

NOTES

FLAVOR ENHANCERS: Top the salad with chopped herbs like dill, cilantro, or parsley for an added burst of freshness. A bit of orange zest in the dressing can also brighten the flavors.

NUTRITIONAL ANALYSIS

PER SERVING: 490 calories; 25 g fat; 37 g carbohydrates; 8 g dietary fiber; 10 g sugars; 35 g protein

The Build Your Bowl System Profile

- **NON-STARCHY VEGETABLES:** Spinach, onion
- **FRUITS:** Orange, grapefruit, avocado
- **WHOLE FOOD FATS:** Salmon, avocado, olive oil
- **HIGH-QUALITY PROTEINS:** Salmon, dressing
- **FIBER-RICH STARCHES:** Lentils
- **FLAVOR ENHANCERS:** Dressing

Mediterranean Tuna & White Bean Salad

This heart-healthy Mediterranean bowl features protein-rich tuna, fiber-packed white beans, and a colorful mix of fresh veggies, all tossed in a zesty lemon oregano vinaigrette.

YIELD: 4 servings • **PREP TIME:** 15 minutes • **COOK TIME:** 0 minutes • **TOTAL TIME:** 15 minutes

FOR THE LEMON OREGANO VINAIGRETTE:

3 tablespoons (45 ml) extra-virgin olive oil
2 tablespoons (30 ml) fresh lemon juice
1 teaspoon red wine vinegar
1 teaspoon dried oregano
1 clove garlic, minced
Salt and pepper, to taste

FOR THE BOWL:

2 cans (8½ ounces, or 240 g, each) albacore tuna, drained
1 can (15 ounces, or 425 g) white beans (cannellini or navy), rinsed and drained
1 small cucumber, diced
¼ small red onion, thinly sliced
1 cup (150 g) cherry tomatoes, halved
¼ cup (33 g) Kalamata olives, pitted and halved
¼ cup (15 g) fresh parsley, chopped
6 to 8 cups (120 to 160 g) arugula
¼ cup (38 g) crumbled feta cheese (optional)
2 tablespoons (17 g) capers, drained (optional)

MAKE THE DRESSING: In a small bowl, shaker, or mason jar, combine all the dressing ingredients. Whisk or shake until well mixed. Adjust the seasoning to taste.

TOSS THE BEAN AND TUNA SALAD: In a large bowl, combine the tuna, beans, cucumber, onion, tomatoes, olives, parsely, and arugula. Toss gently to mix.

BUILD THE BOWL: Pour the dressing over the salad and toss to coat all ingredients evenly. If desired, sprinkle with feta cheese and capers for extra flavor. Serve immediately.

NOTES

STARCH ALTERNATIVES: Swap out white beans for chickpeas, lentils, or quinoa for a different texture and flavor, while still keeping the dish heart healthy and fiber rich.

FLAVOR ENHANCERS: For a flavor boost, consider adding fresh herbs like basil, mint, or dill. You can also include a splash of balsamic vinegar or a sprinkle of sumac for extra zest.

NUTRITIONAL ANALYSIS

PER SERVING: 445 calories; 17 g fat; 33 g carbohydrates; 9 g dietary fiber; 4 g sugars; 41 g protein

The Build Your Bowl System Profile

- NON-STARCHY VEGETABLES: Arugula, cucumber, onion, tomatoes
- FRUITS: Olives
- WHOLE FOOD FATS: Tuna, olives, cheese, olive oil
- HIGH-QUALITY PROTEINS: Tuna, cheese
- FIBER-RICH STARCHES: White beans
- FLAVOR ENHANCERS: Cheese, capers, dressing

Sunrise Quinoa Bowl with Scrambled Tofu

A hearty mix of quinoa, sweet potatoes, and scrambled tofu, this plant-based bowl offers the perfect balance of nutrition to fuel your morning or midday.

YIELD: 4 servings • **PREP TIME:** 20 minutes • **COOK TIME:** 25 minutes • **TOTAL TIME:** 45 minutes

FOR THE CITRUS-MUSTARD VINAIGRETTE:

2 tablespoons (30 ml) extra-virgin olive oil
1 tablespoon (15 ml) fresh lemon juice
1 tablespoon (15 ml) fresh orange juice
1 teaspoon Dijon mustard
½ teaspoon pure maple syrup, or more to taste
Salt and pepper, to taste

FOR THE BOWL:

2 medium sweet potatoes, peeled and cubed
1 tablespoon (15 ml) extra-virgin olive oil
Salt and pepper, to taste
1 cup (100 g) cremini mushrooms, sliced
1 clove garlic, minced
1 red bell pepper, cored and diced
½ red onion, thinly sliced
1 block (7 ounces, or 200 g) firm tofu, crumbled
½ teaspoon turmeric powder
½ teaspoon smoked paprika
2 tablespoons (15 g) nutritional yeast
4 to 6 cups (120 to 180 g) baby spinach
½ cup (43 g) cooked quinoa
½ avocado, sliced

MAKE THE DRESSING: Add all the dressing ingredients to a small bowl, shaker, or mason jar. Whisk or shake until well mixed.

ROAST THE SWEET POTATOES: Preheat the oven to 400°F (200°C). Toss the sweet potatoes with olive oil, salt, and pepper. Spread on a parchment-lined baking sheet and roast for 20 to 25 minutes until golden and tender. Set aside.

SAUTÉ THE VEGETABLES: Heat a skillet over medium heat. Sauté the mushrooms and garlic for 5 to 7 minutes until tender. Add the bell pepper and onion, cooking for another 3 to 4 minutes. Season with salt and pepper. Set aside.

SCRAMBLE THE TOFU: In the same skillet, cook the tofu with the turmeric, paprika, and nutritional yeast for 5 to 7 minutes, stirring occasionally, until browned. Add the vegetables and sweet potatoes, tossing to combine. Remove from the heat.

BUILD THE BOWL: Toss the spinach with a little dressing in a medium bowl. Divide among four bowls, top each with quinoa and the tofu mixture. Garnish with avocado, drizzle with more dressing to taste, and serve.

NOTES

BRING THE CRUNCH: Sprinkle on toasted nuts or seeds, such as pumpkin or sunflower seeds, for added texture, satisfying crunch, and even more nutrients.

ENHANCE THE FLAVOR: Cook the quinoa in low-sodium vegetable broth instead of water for a richer, more savory base.

NUTRITIONAL ANALYSIS

PER SERVING: 355 calories; 17 g fat; 39 g carbohydrates; 8 g dietary fiber; 8 g sugars; 13 g protein

The Build Your Bowl System Profile

- **NON-STARCHY VEGETABLES:** Spinach, bell pepper, onion, mushrooms
- **WHOLE FOOD FATS:** Avocado, olive oil
- **HIGH-QUALITY PROTEINS:** Tofu, quinoa
- **FIBER-RICH STARCHES:** Sweet potatoes, quinoa
- **FLAVOR ENHANCERS:** Dressing

Apricot Almond Couscous Bowl

This refreshing bowl features fiber-rich whole wheat couscous with crisp vegetables, sweet apricots, and fresh herbs for an antioxidant boost, all brought together by a bright lemon dressing.

YIELD: 4 servings • **PREP TIME:** 15 minutes • **COOK TIME:** 20 minutes • **TOTAL TIME:** 35 minutes

FOR THE SUNNY LEMON SPICE DRESSING:

3 tablespoons (45 ml) extra-virgin olive oil
3 tablespoons (45 ml) fresh lemon juice
1 tablespoon (20 g) pure honey or maple syrup
1 teaspoon Dijon mustard
½ teaspoon ground cumin
¼ teaspoon ground cinnamon
¼ teaspoon ground coriander
½ teaspoon garlic powder
Salt and pepper, to taste

FOR THE BOWL:

1¼ cups (300 ml) water or low-sodium vegetable broth
1 cup (170 g) whole wheat couscous
½ cup (75 g) dried apricots, chopped
½ cup (60 g) toasted almonds, sliced
½ cucumber, diced
½ red bell pepper, diced
¼ red onion, thinly sliced
¼ cup (15 g) fresh parsley, chopped
¼ cup (24 g) fresh mint, chopped
4 to 6 cups (80 to 120 g) baby arugula or mixed greens

MAKE THE DRESSING: In a small bowl, shaker, or mason jar, combine all the dressing ingredients. Whisk or shake until well mixed.

COOK THE COUSCOUS: In a medium saucepan, bring the water to a boil. Stir in the couscous, cover, and remove from the heat. Let it sit for 5 minutes. After 5 minutes, fluff the couscous with a fork to separate the grains.

BUILD THE BOWL: In a large bowl, combine the couscous, apricots, almonds, cucumber, bell pepper, onion, parsley, and mint. Drizzle some dressing over the mixture and toss until everything is evenly coated.

SERVE: Divide the baby arugula among four bowls. For more even coating, toss lightly with a bit of dressing, or simply drizzle dressing over the top for a more visual presentation. Spoon the couscous mixture over the greens. Serve immediately.

NOTES

FLAVORFUL FLEXIBILITY: This bowl is versatile and can be enjoyed warm or chilled. For added protein, consider topping with grilled chicken, tofu, or roasted chickpeas. It also pairs well with a side of hummus or a light yogurt-based dip for extra flavor and nutrition.

REDUCE THE SUGAR: Use half the honey or maple syrup in the dressing, adding a few drops of stevia or monk fruit to keep the sweetness without extra sugar.

NUTRITIONAL ANALYSIS

PER SERVING: 390 calories; 17 g fat; 53 g carbohydrates; 6 g dietary fiber; 14 g sugars; 10 g protein

The Build Your Bowl System Profile

- NON-STARCHY VEGETABLES: Arugula or mixed greens, cucumber, bell pepper, red onion
- FRUITS: Dried apricots
- WHOLE FOOD FATS: Almonds, olive oil
- FIBER-RICH STARCHES: Couscous
- FLAVOR ENHANCERS: Dried apricots, herbs, dressing

Chicken & Roasted Beet Kale Salad

Combining juicy chicken, earthy beets, and crisp kale, this vibrant, nutrient-packed bowl is rich in antioxidants and full of fresh flavors.

YIELD: 4 servings • **PREP TIME:** 15 minutes • **COOK TIME:** 50 minutes • **TOTAL TIME:** 1 hour 5 minutes

FOR THE LEMON TAHINI DRESSING:

⅓ cup (80 g) tahini
3 tablespoons (45 ml) fresh lemon juice
1 tablespoon (20 g) pure maple syrup or honey
2 cloves garlic, minced
3 to 4 tablespoons (45 to 60 ml) water, as needed
Salt and pepper, to taste

FOR THE BOWL:

2 medium beets, cleaned, trimmed, and halved
1 to 2 tablespoons (15 to 30 ml) extra-virgin olive oil
Salt and pepper, to taste
2 medium boneless, skinless chicken breasts (about 14 ounces, or 400 g, total)
1 teaspoon garlic powder
8 cups (535 g) chopped stemmed kale
1 large carrot, shredded
1 cup (160 g) fresh pomegranate seeds
¼ cup (40 g) toasted pepitas
¼ cup (38 g) crumbled goat cheese (optional)

MAKE THE DRESSING: In a small bowl, whisk together the tahini, lemon juice, maple syrup, garlic, and water until smooth. Add water as needed for your desired consistency. Season with salt and pepper.

PREPARE THE BEETS: Preheat the oven to 400°F (200°C). Place the beets in a lightly greased baking dish, drizzle with olive oil, and season with salt and pepper. Cover the dish with foil and roast for 50 to 60 minutes, or until tender. Let the beets cool for 5 to 10 minutes before peeling (or leave the skins on). Slice into cubes and set aside.

COOK THE CHICKEN: While the beets roast, season the chicken breasts with salt, pepper, and garlic powder. Heat a grill pan or non-stick skillet over medium-high heat. If the pan is not non-stick or appears dry, add the olive oil. Cook the chicken for 6 to 7 minutes per side, or until the internal temperature reaches 165°F (74°C). Let rest for 5 minutes before slicing.

PREPARE THE KALE: Rinse the kale under cool water while massaging the leaves to soften. Drain well and transfer to a large bowl. Pour half the dressing over and massage the kale for 1 to 2 minutes until tender and evenly coated.

BUILD THE BOWL: Layer the beets, carrot, and pomegranate seeds over the dressed kale. Drizzle with additional dressing to taste, then gently toss to combine. Divide the salad among four bowls, and top with chicken, pepitas, and goat cheese, if using. Serve immediately.

NOTES

CUSTOMIZE YOUR PROTEIN: Swap the chicken with grilled tofu or tempeh.

FLAVOR ENHANCERS: Add fresh parsley or mint for extra flavor and freshness.

NUTRITIONAL ANALYSIS

PER SERVING: 440 calories; 23 g fat; 29 g carbohydrates; 7 g dietary fiber; 15 g sugars; 33 g protein

The Build Your Bowl System Profile

- NON-STARCHY VEGETABLES: Kale, beets, carrot
- FRUITS: Pomegranate seeds
- WHOLE FOOD FATS: Pepitas, cheese, olive oil, tahini
- HIGH-QUALITY PROTEINS: Chicken, cheese
- FLAVOR ENHANCERS: Cheese, dressing

Seared Salmon & Mixed Berry Salad

Packed with omega-3s and antioxidants, salmon and berries create a powerhouse duo for heart health. Toss in fresh spinach and a refreshingly sweet raspberry vinaigrette, and you've got a nutrient-rich, flavor-packed bowl that's perfect for any meal.

YIELD: 4 servings • **PREP TIME:** 15 minutes plus 15 minutes to marinate • **COOK TIME:** 10 minutes • **TOTAL TIME:** 40 minutes

FOR THE SALMON:

1 to 2 tablespoons (15 to 30 ml) fresh lemon juice
1 tablespoon (15 ml) extra-virgin olive oil
2 teaspoons garlic powder
1 teaspoon smoked paprika (optional)
Salt and pepper, to taste
4 wild-caught, skinless salmon fillets (about 4 ounces, or 115 g, each)

FOR THE RASPBERRY VINAIGRETTE:

⅓ cup (80 ml) extra-virgin olive oil
2 tablespoons (40 g) raspberry jam (ideally one with no added sugar)
2 tablespoons (30 ml) balsamic vinegar
1 to 2 tablespoons (15 to 30 ml) water, as needed
1 tablespoon (11 g) Dijon mustard
1 tablespoon (2 g) fresh basil, finely chopped
Salt and pepper, to taste

FOR THE BOWL:

8 cups (240 g) baby spinach
1 cup (150 g) blackberries
1 cup (150 g) blueberries
1 cup (150 g) strawberries, hulled and sliced
¼ cup (38 g) crumbled feta cheese (optional)
¼ cup (10 g) fresh basil, finely chopped
¼ cup (30 g) toasted walnuts, chopped

PREPARE THE SALMON: In a small bowl, whisk together the lemon juice, olive oil, garlic powder, paprika, and salt and pepper. Place the fillets in a shallow dish, pour the marinade over them, and coat evenly. Cover and marinate in the fridge for 15 to 30 minutes. Preheat a skillet over medium-high heat. Add the fillets to the skillet and sear for 4 to 5 minutes per side, or until the salmon is cooked through and flakes easily with a fork. Remove from the heat and let rest for a few minutes.

MAKE THE DRESSING: In a small bowl, whisk together the olive oil, jam, vinegar, water (as needed), mustard, and basil until well combined. Season with salt and pepper to taste. Adjust the consistency by adding more water if necessary.

BUILD THE BOWL: In a large serving bowl, layer the baby spinach with blackberries, blueberries, and strawberries. Drizzle with dressing and toss gently to coat. Divide the salad among four bowls, top each with a salmon fillet, and sprinkle with feta, fresh basil, and walnuts, if using. Serve immediately.

NOTES

MAKE IT YOUR OWN: For added variety, swap the walnuts for toasted pecans or sunflower seeds, or try goat cheese instead of feta for a different flavor profile.

NUTRITIONAL ANALYSIS

PER SERVING: 520 calories; 35 g fat; 25 g carbohydrates; 6 g dietary fiber; 14 g sugars; 31 g protein

The Build Your Bowl System Profile

- NON-STARCHY VEGETABLES: Spinach
- FRUITS: Berries
- WHOLE FOOD FATS: Salmon, walnuts, olive oil, cheese
- HIGH-QUALITY PROTEINS: Salmon, cheese
- FLAVOR ENHANCERS: Basil, cheese, marinade, dressing

Fire-Roasted Tomato & Basil Bulgur Bowl

The perfect balance of flavors and textures, this bowl combines smoky fire-roasted tomatoes, tender squash, and earthy bulgur with a sweet basil balsamic vinaigrette.

YIELD: 4 servings • **PREP TIME:** 15 minutes • **COOK TIME:** 25 minutes • **TOTAL TIME:** 40 minutes

FOR THE SWEET BASIL BALSAMIC VINAIGRETTE:

3 to 4 tablespoons (45 to 60 ml) white balsamic vinegar
¼ cup (60 ml) extra-virgin olive oil
1 tablespoon (11 g) Dijon mustard
1 tablespoon (20 g) pure honey or maple syrup, or to taste
1 clove garlic, minced
1 tablespoon (2 g) fresh basil, finely chopped
Salt and pepper, to taste

FOR THE BOWL:

4 Roma tomatoes, halved
1 medium yellow squash, thinly sliced
1 tablespoon (15 ml) extra-virgin olive oil
Salt and pepper, to taste
½ teaspoon dried oregano or thyme
2 cloves garlic, minced
1 cup (180 g) bulgur
2 cups (480 ml) water or low-sodium vegetable broth
1 cup (40 g) fresh basil leaves, torn or chopped
½ small red onion, thinly sliced
1 medium cucumber, diced
⅓ cup (50 g) crumbled goat cheese
¼ cup (30 g) toasted pistachios, roughly chopped

MAKE THE DRESSING: In a small bowl, whisk together 3 tablespoons (45 ml) vinegar, the olive oil, mustard, honey, garlic, and basil. Taste and add more vinegar, if desired. Season with salt and pepper.

ROAST THE TOMATOES AND SQUASH: Preheat the oven to 400°F (200°C). Place the tomato halves and squash on a baking sheet. Drizzle with the olive oil, sprinkle with salt, pepper, oregano, and toss with the garlic. Roast for 20 to 25 minutes until the tomatoes are slightly charred and softened, and the squash is tender. Set aside to cool slightly.

COOK THE BULGUR: Rinse the bulgur under cold water. In a medium saucepan, bring the water to a boil. Add the bulgur, reduce the heat to low, cover, and simmer for 12 to 15 minutes, or until tender and the liquid is absorbed. Fluff with a fork and set aside to cool.

BUILD THE BOWL: In a large bowl, combine the cooled bulgur, squash, basil, onion, and cucumber. Drizzle the dressing to taste over the mixture and toss gently to coat. Divide the bulgur mixture among four bowls. Top each with tomato halves, goat cheese, and pistachios. Serve immediately with additional dressing on the side.

NOTES

BOOST THE PROTEIN: Add grilled chicken, shrimp, seared salmon, marinated tofu, or tempeh.

MAKE IT VEGAN: Replace the goat cheese with creamy avocado slices or nutritional yeast for a cheesy flavor, or toasted hemp seeds for extra plant-based protein.

NUTRITIONAL ANALYSIS

PER SERVING: 425 calories; 24 g fat; 46 g carbohydrates; 8 g dietary fiber; 13 g sugars; 10 g protein

The Build Your Bowl System Profile

- **NON-STARCHY VEGETABLES:** Tomatoes, squash, cucumber, onion, basil
- **WHOLE FOOD FATS:** Cheese, pistachios, olive oil
- **HIGH-QUALITY PROTEINS:** Cheese
- **STARCHES:** Bulgur
- **FLAVOR ENHANCERS:** Seasonings, dressing

Wholesome Mixed Greens Quinoa Bowl

An explosion of fresh flavors, this feel-good meal features layers of greens, quinoa, and colorful veggies, all tossed in a zesty herb vinaigrette and topped with crunchy nuts and seeds.

YIELD: 4 servings • **PREP TIME:** 15 minutes • **COOK TIME:** 20 minutes • **TOTAL TIME:** 35 minutes

FOR THE HERBACEOUS BALSAMIC VINAIGRETTE:

¼ cup (60 ml) balsamic vinegar
3 tablespoons (45 ml) extra-virgin olive oil
2 tablespoons (30 ml) water or low-sodium vegetable broth
1 tablespoon (11 g) Dijon mustard
1 tablespoon (20 g) pure maple syrup or honey, or more to taste
1 tablespoon (2 g) fresh basil, finely chopped
1 tablespoon (4 g) fresh parsley, finely chopped
1 clove garlic, minced
Salt and pepper, to taste

FOR THE BOWL:

1 cup (170 g) quinoa (tricolored if available)
2 cups (480 ml) water or low-sodium vegetable broth
6 to 8 cups (330 to 440 g) mixed greens, roughly chopped
Salt and pepper, to taste
2 medium bell peppers (red and yellow), thinly sliced
1 medium carrot, julienned or shredded
1 medium zucchini, spiralized or thinly sliced
2 or 3 medium Roma tomatoes, diced and seeded
1 cucumber, diced
1 avocado, peeled, pitted, and sliced
¼ cup (30 g) toasted sunflower seeds
¼ cup (30 g) toasted walnuts, crushed
¼ cup (15 g) fresh parsley, chopped

MAKE THE DRESSING: In a small bowl, shaker, or mason jar, combine all the dressing ingredients. Whisk or shake until well mixed. Adjust the seasoning with salt and pepper to taste.

COOK THE QUINOA: Rinse and drain the quinoa. In a medium saucepan, combine it with the water. Bring to a boil over medium heat, then reduce the heat, cover, and simmer until the liquid is absorbed, 15 to 20 minutes. Fluff with a fork and set aside to cool.

BUILD THE BOWL: In a large bowl, season the greens with salt and pepper. Drizzle with dressing and toss to coat. Add the bell peppers, carrots, zucchini, tomatoes, and cucumber to the dressed greens. If desired, drizzle with additional dressing and toss gently. Add the quinoa and toss gently again to mix.

SERVE: Divide the salad among four bowls. Top each with avocado, sunflower seeds, walnuts, and parsley. Serve immediately for the freshest flavor and texture.

NOTES

BOOST THE PROTEIN: Add grilled chicken, salmon, or shrimp. For a plant-based option, try grilled tofu, tempeh bacon, or edamame.

FLAVOR ENHANCERS: For a savory twist, sprinkle with crumbled feta or add a few olives.

NUTRITIONAL ANALYSIS

PER SERVING: 490 calories; 28 g fat; 51 g carbohydrates; 10 g dietary fiber; 12 g sugars; 12 g protein

The Build Your Bowl System Profile

- NON-STARCHY VEGETABLES: Mixed greens, bell peppers, carrot, zucchini, tomatoes, cucumber
- FRUITS: Avocado
- WHOLE FOOD FATS: Avocado, sunflower seeds, walnuts, olive oil
- HIGH-QUALITY PROTEINS: Quinoa
- FIBER-RICH STARCHES: Quinoa
- FLAVOR ENHANCERS: Parsley, dressing

Tangy Lentil & Pomegranate Bowl

This refreshing bowl brings together tender lentils, creamy avocado, juicy pomegranate seeds, and a tangy apple cider vinaigrette for a delicious balance of flavors and textures.

YIELD: 4 servings • **PREP TIME:** 15 minutes • **COOK TIME:** 25 minutes • **TOTAL TIME:** 40 minutes

FOR THE APPLE CIDER VINAIGRETTE:

¼ cup (60 ml) extra-virgin olive oil
2 tablespoons (30 ml) apple cider vinegar
1 tablespoon (11 g) Dijon mustard
1 tablespoon (20 g) pure honey or maple syrup
1 clove garlic, minced
1 tablespoon (3 g) fresh Italian parsley, finely chopped
Salt and pepper, to taste

FOR THE BOWL:

1 cup (180 g) green lentils
3 cups (720 ml) water or low-sodium vegetable broth
6 cups (180 g) baby spinach, roughly chopped
1 large cucumber, diced
½ small red onion, diced
½ cup (80 g) fresh pomegranate seeds
¼ cup (30 g) fresh Italian parsley, chopped
1 avocado, peeled, pitted, and diced
¼ cup (40 g) toasted pepitas
Salt and pepper, to taste

MAKE THE DRESSING: Add all the dressing ingredients to a small bowl, shaker, or mason jar. Whisk or shake until well blended. Adjust salt and pepper to taste.

COOK THE LENTILS: Rinse the lentils under cold water. Add to a medium saucepan with the water. Bring to a boil over medium heat, then reduce the heat, cover, and simmer for 20 to 25 minutes, or until tender. Drain any excess liquid and set aside to cool.

BUILD THE BOWL: In a large bowl, toss the spinach with a drizzle of dressing until well coated. Add the cucumber, onion, pomegranate seeds, parsley, and lentils. Gently fold in the diced avocado and pepitas. Drizzle with more dressing to taste and toss gently to combine. Serve immediately for the freshest flavor.

NOTES

COMPLETE THE PROTEIN: Add grilled chicken for a lean boost, baked tofu for a plant-based option, or quinoa for a hearty, protein-rich grain. Feta or goat cheese adds tangy creaminess with extra protein.

FLAVOR ENHANCERS: Fresh herbs like mint, dill, or basil brighten the salad, while lemon juice or zest adds citrusy freshness. For a little kick, try red pepper flakes or smoked paprika.

NUTRITIONAL ANALYSIS

PER SERVING: 455 calories; 24 g fat; 48 g carbohydrates; 11 g dietary fiber; 10 g sugars; 17 g protein

The Build Your Bowl System Profile

- **NON-STARCHY VEGETABLES:** Spinach, cucumber, onion
- **FRUITS:** Pomegranate seeds, avocado
- **WHOLE FOOD FATS:** Avocado, pepitas, olive oil
- **FIBER-RICH STARCHES:** Lentils
- **FLAVOR ENHANCERS:** Parsley, dressing

Cantaloupe & Blueberry Shrimp Salad

Featuring marinated shrimp, sweet cantaloupe, and fresh blueberries, all tossed in a honey-lime vinaigrette, this salad is rich in antioxidants, healthy fats, and fiber.

YIELD: 4 servings • **PREP TIME:** 20 minutes • **COOK TIME:** 5 minutes • **TOTAL TIME:** 25 minutes

FOR THE SHRIMP:

2 tablespoons (30 ml) fresh lime juice
1 tablespoon (15 ml) extra-virgin olive oil
2 cloves garlic, minced
1 teaspoon smoked paprika
½ teaspoon ground cumin
½ teaspoon honey
Salt and pepper, to taste
1 pound (450 g) large shrimp (13 to 15 count), peeled and deveined

FOR THE HONEY LIME VINAIGRETTE:

¼ cup (60 ml) extra-virgin olive oil
3 tablespoons (45 ml) fresh lime juice, or to taste
4½ teaspoons (22 ml) white balsamic vinegar
1 to 2 tablespoons (20 to 40 g) pure honey, or to taste
1 teaspoon lime zest
Salt and pepper, to taste

FOR THE BOWL:

6 cups (330 g) mixed greens
2 cups (300 g) cantaloupe, cubed
1½ cups (225 g) blueberries
1 medium cucumber, thinly sliced
½ small red onion, thinly sliced
1 large avocado, peeled, pitted, and sliced
¼ cup (38 g) crumbled feta or goat cheese
¼ cup (30 g) toasted walnuts or almonds, roughly chopped
2 tablespoons (12 g) fresh mint leaves, chopped (optional)

PREPARE THE SHRIMP: In a medium bowl, whisk together all the marinade ingredients, add the shrimp, and toss to coat. Cover and refrigerate for 15 to 20 minutes. Preheat a grill or grill pan over medium-high heat. Skewer the shrimp or place them directly on the grill, cooking 2 to 3 minutes per side until pink and opaque. Set aside.

MAKE THE DRESSING: In a small bowl, shaker, or mason jar, combine all the dressing ingredients. Whisk or shake until well blended. Taste the dressing and adjust the sweetness or acidity as needed, then whisk or shake again to fully combine.

BUILD THE BOWL: In a large salad bowl, toss the mixed greens with a drizzle of dressing until coated. Add the cantaloupe, blueberries, cucumber, and onion and gently toss to combine. Divide the salad among four bowls and top each with shrimp, avocado, cheese, nuts, and mint (if using). Serve immediately, with extra dressing on the side, if desired.

NOTES

CUSTOMIZE YOUR PROTEIN: Swap the shrimp with grilled chicken breast, seared salmon, or even tofu or tempeh for a plant-based alternative.

FLAVOR ENHANCERS: Add a sprinkle of red pepper flakes or a drizzle of balsamic glaze for a little extra kick and sweetness.

NUTRITIONAL ANALYSIS

PER SERVING: 490 calories; 30 g fat; 32 g carbohydrates; 7 g dietary fiber; 20 g sugars; 28 g protein

The Build Your Bowl System Profile

- NON-STARCHY VEGETABLES: Mixed greens, cucumber, onion
- FRUITS: Cantaloupe, blueberries, avocado
- WHOLE FOOD FATS: Avocado, nuts, cheese, olive oil
- HIGH-QUALITY PROTEINS: Shrimp, cheese
- FLAVOR ENHANCERS: Mint, marinade, dressing

Trout Farro Bowl with Mango Salsa

This protein-packed bowl is a nutritional powerhouse and a real feast for the senses. The mild, tender trout, nutty farro, and refreshing mango salsa, complemented by creamy avocado, deliver a mouth-watering blend of quality fats, fiber, and vibrant flavors, leaving you feeling energized and satisfied.

YIELD: 4 servings • **PREP TIME:** 20 minutes • **COOK TIME:** 25 minutes • **TOTAL TIME:** 45 minutes

FOR THE MANGO SALSA:

1 ripe mango, peeled and diced
1 red bell pepper, diced
1 cucumber, seeded and diced
½ red onion, finely diced, or more to taste
1 jalapeño pepper, seeded and finely chopped
¼ cup (4 g) fresh cilantro, chopped
2 tablespoons (30 ml) fresh lime juice
1 tablespoon (15 ml) extra-virgin olive oil
Salt and pepper, to taste

FOR THE BOWL:

1 pound (450 g) trout, filleted
1 teaspoon garlic powder
2 tablespoons (30 ml) fresh lime juice, plus wedges for squeezing
Salt and pepper, to taste
1 cup (200 g) farro
2 cups (480 ml) water or low-sodium vegetable broth
1 avocado, sliced

MAKE THE SALSA: Combine the mango, bell pepper, cucumber, red onion, jalapeño, and cilantro in a medium bowl. Add the lime juice and olive oil, then toss gently. Season with salt and pepper. Refrigerate for 15 to 20 minutes to meld the flavors.

PREPARE THE TROUT: Preheat thc oven to 375°F (190°C). Season the fillets with the garlic powder, lime juice, salt, and pepper. Place on a baking sheet lined with parchment paper. Bake for 12 to 15 minutes, or until the trout flakes easily with a fork. Let cool slightly, then flake into large chunks.

COOK THE FARRO: Rinse the farro under cold water. In a medium saucepan, combine the farro with the water. Bring to a boil over medium-high heat, then reduce to a simmer, cover, and cook until the farro is tender and the liquid is absorbed, 20 to 25 minutes. Fluff with a fork and set aside.

BUILD THE BOWL: In a large bowl, gently toss the farro with the mango salsa. Divide among four bowls and top with trout and avocado. For added flavor, squeeze fresh lime juice over each bowl. Serve immediately.

NOTES

GRAIN ALTERNATIVES: Substitute farro with quinoa, brown rice, or barley if preferred.

FLAVOR ENHANCERS: Add some roasted nuts or seeds for extra crunch and nutrition.

NUTRITIONAL ANALYSIS

PER SERVING: 448 calories; 13 g fat; 54 g carbohydrates; 8 g dietary fiber; 15 g sugars; 32 g protein

The Build Your Bowl System Profile

- NON-STARCHY VEGETABLES: Bell pepper, cucumber, onion
- FRUITS: Avocado, mango
- WHOLE FOOD FATS: Trout, avocado, olive oil
- HIGH-QUALITY PROTEINS: Trout
- FIBER-RICH STARCHES: Farro
- FLAVOR ENHANCERS: Cilantro, jalapeño pepper, dressing

Kale Caesar Salad with Crispy Chickpeas

A nutritious twist on the classic Caesar, this simple, savory salad bowl is loaded with fiber, protein, and health-promoting fats.

YIELD: 4 servings • **PREP TIME:** 15 minutes • **COOK TIME:** 25 minutes • **TOTAL TIME:** 40 minutes

FOR THE CHICKPEAS:

1 can (15 ounces, or 425 g) chickpeas, drained, rinsed, and patted dry
1 tablespoon (15 ml) extra-virgin olive oil
1 teaspoon smoked paprika
1 teaspoon garlic powder
Salt and pepper, to taste
¼ teaspoon cayenne pepper (optional)
1 tablespoon (8 g) cornstarch or tapioca flour (optional)

FOR THE CREAMY CAESAR DRESSING:

½ cup (120 g) plain Greek yogurt (whole milk or 2% reduced fat)
2 tablespoons (30 ml) fresh lemon juice
1 to 2 tablespoons (15 to 30 ml) extra-virgin olive oil
2 or 3 anchovy fillets, mashed
1 or 2 cloves garlic, minced
1 teaspoon Dijon mustard
1 teaspoon Worcestershire sauce
2 tablespoons (15 g) grated Parmesan cheese (optional)
1 to 2 tablespoons (15 to 30 ml) water, as needed
Salt and pepper, to taste

FOR THE BOWL:

8 cups (535 g) chopped stemmed kale
1 medium cucumber, thinly sliced
2 small carrots, thinly sliced
1 cup (150 g) cherry tomatoes, halved
¼ cup (30 g) toasted walnuts, roughly chopped
2 tablespoons (15 g) grated Parmesan cheese

PREPARE THE CHICKPEAS: Preheat the oven to 400°F (200°C). Remove the loose skins from the chickpeas, then let sit for 10 to 15 minutes to air-dry, which helps them absorb flavors and crisp up. Toss with the olive oil, paprika, garlic powder, salt, pepper, and cayenne (if using). For crispier chickpeas, sprinkle with the optional cornstarch and toss again to coat. Spread on a parchment-lined baking sheet and roast for 20 to 25 minutes, shaking halfway through, until crispy and golden brown. Set aside to cool slightly.

MAKE THE DRESSING: Combine all the dressing ingredients in a blender or food processor. Blend on low speed, gradually increasing the speed until smooth. Alternatively, whisk the ingredients together in a small bowl until well combined.

BUILD THE BOWL: In a large bowl, toss the kale with half the dressing, massaging to soften. Add the cucumber, carrots, tomatoes, and walnuts and toss to combine. Divide among four bowls, top with the chickpeas and Parmesan, and drizzle with more dressing if desired. Serve immediately.

NOTES

MAKE IT YOUR OWN: Swap the chickpeas with grilled chicken, tofu, or tempeh for a different protein option. You can also replace the walnuts with almonds, sunflower seeds, or pepitas for a different crunch.

NUTRITIONAL ANALYSIS

PER SERVING: 340 calories; 19 g fat; 30 g carbohydrates; 9 g dietary fiber; 7 g sugars; 17 g protein

The Build Your Bowl System Profile

- NON-STARCHY VEGETABLES: Kale, cucumber, carrots, tomatoes
- WHOLE FOOD FATS: Walnuts, cheese, yogurt, olive oil
- HIGH-QUALITY PROTEINS: Cheese, yogurt
- FIBER-RICH STARCHES: Chickpeas
- FLAVOR ENHANCERS: Cheese, seasonings, dressing

8

Revitalizing Detox & Anti-Inflammatory Bowls

As we reach the final chapter, it's only fitting to focus on something that ties everything together—helping your body reset, recover, and thrive. Chronic inflammation can lead to fatigue, discomfort, and various health issues, especially with hectic schedules, poor sleep, and occasional overindulgences. That's where this chapter comes in, offering bowls that provide extra support to help you feel your best, inside and out.

What sets these bowls apart is their focus on ingredients known for their anti-inflammatory and detox-supporting properties.

For example, the Turmeric Quinoa and Edamame Bowl (page 163) blends turmeric's powerful benefits with protein-packed edamame and fresh veggies.

For something refreshing, the Citrus Herb Marinated–Mushroom Salad (page 169) combines marinated mushrooms with crisp veggies and a zesty citrus vinaigrette.

For a heartier option, the Moroccan Carrot Bowl with Lentils (page 157) brings together spiced carrots, fiber-rich lentils, and a creamy yogurt dressing.

Then there's the Ginger Brussels Sprout Slaw (page 152), delivering rejuvenating crunch with shredded Brussels sprouts, carrots, and red cabbage, all dressed in a tangy ginger lime sauce

Whether you're trying to bounce back after a stressful week, boost your energy, or simply enjoy lighter, more nutrient-packed meals, these recipes will help calm inflammation and support your body's natural processes, all while keeping you satisfied and energized.

Ginger Brussels Sprout Slaw

Not your typical slaw, this combination of freshly shaved Brussels sprouts, carrots, and a tangy ginger lime dressing delivers a powerful trifecta of anti-inflammatory, antioxidant, and detoxifying benefits.

YIELD: 4 servings • **PREP TIME:** 15 minutes • **COOK TIME:** 0 minutes • **TOTAL TIME:** 15 minutes

FOR THE GINGER LIME DRESSING:

¼ cup (60 ml) toasted sesame oil
2 tablespoons (30 ml) rice vinegar
2 tablespoons (30 ml) fresh lime juice
1 tablespoon (20 g) pure honey
1 tablespoon (15 ml) soy sauce or tamari
1 tablespoon (8 g) grated fresh ginger
1 clove garlic, minced
Salt and pepper, to taste

FOR THE BOWL:

4 cups (400 g) Brussels sprouts, shredded
2 medium carrots, shredded
½ small red cabbage, shredded
½ red bell pepper, thinly sliced
¼ cup (15 g) fresh parsley, chopped
4 scallions with tops and bulbs, thinly sliced
¼ cup (40 g) toasted pepitas

MAKE THE DRESSING: Add all the dressing ingredients to a small bowl, shaker, or mason jar. Whisk or shake until well mixed. Adjust the seasoning to taste.

BUILD THE BOWL: In a large bowl, combine the Brussels sprouts, carrots, cabbage, bell pepper, parsley, and scallions. Pour the dressing over the mixture and toss gently until everything is evenly coated.

SERVE: Divide the slaw among four bowls and sprinkle each with pepitas. Serve immediately as a refreshing side dish or a light stand-alone meal.

NOTES

OPTIONAL BLANCHING: For a slightly milder flavor and softer texture, blanch the Brussels sprouts in boiling water for 1 to 2 minutes before shredding them.

ADD SOME PROTEIN: Add grilled chicken, shrimp, or tofu to make this slaw a more filling main course.

FLAVOR ENHANCERS: Fresh herbs like cilantro or Thai basil can add a burst of freshness to the slaw.

NUTRITIONAL ANALYSIS

PER SERVING: 330 calories; 18 g fat; 39 g carbohydrates; 9 g dietary fiber; 18 g sugars; 9 g protein

The Build Your Bowl System Profile

- **NON-STARCHY VEGETABLES:** Brussels sprouts, carrots, cabbage, bell pepper
- **WHOLE FOOD FATS:** Pepitas, sesame oil
- **FLAVOR ENHANCERS:** Parsley, dressing

Berrylicious Green Salad with Cauliflower Rice

This light and flavorful salad delivers a refreshing blend of crisp greens, juicy berries, and tender cauliflower rice, tossed in a tangy berry lemon vinaigrette and topped with crunchy almonds and fresh herbs.

YIELD: 4 servings • **PREP TIME:** 15 minutes • **COOK TIME:** 10 minutes • **TOTAL TIME:** 25 minutes

FOR THE BERRY LEMON VINAIGRETTE:

¼ cup (60 ml) extra-virgin olive oil
2 tablespoons (30 ml) fresh lemon juice
1 to 2 tablespoons (15 to 30 ml) apple cider vinegar
1 tablespoon (20 g) pure honey or maple syrup, or more to taste
¼ cup (weight varies) mixed berries (blueberries, raspberries, strawberries)
1 teaspoon Dijon mustard
Salt and pepper, to taste

FOR THE BOWL:

1 medium head cauliflower, cut into florets
Salt and pepper, to taste
4 to 5 cups (80 to 100 g) arugula, roughly chopped
2 to 3 cups (60 to 90 g) watercress, roughly chopped
½ cup (75 g) blueberries
½ cup (75 g) raspberries
½ cup (75 g) strawberries, hulled and sliced
1 medium cucumber, seeded and diced
½ small red onion, thinly sliced
½ cup (60 g) toasted almonds, sliced
¼ cup (24 g) fresh mint, chopped
¼ cup (10 g) fresh basil, chopped

MAKE THE DRESSING: In a blender or food processor, combine the olive oil, lemon juice, vinegar, honey, mixed berries, and mustard. Blend on low speed, gradually increasing the speed to high speed, until smooth. Taste and season with salt and pepper as needed.

PREPARE THE CAULIFLOWER RICE: Using a food processor, pulse the cauliflower florets until they reach a rice-like texture. In a non-stick skillet over medium heat, cook the cauliflower rice for 5 to 7 minutes, stirring occasionally, until tender. Season with salt and pepper to taste. Allow it to cool completely before adding it to the salad.

BUILD THE BOWL: In a large bowl, combine the arugula, watercress, blueberries, raspberries, strawberries, cucumber, and onion. Add the cauliflower rice and toss gently to mix. Drizzle with dressing and toss again until everything is evenly coated. Divide the salad evenly among four bowls. Top each with almonds, mint, and basil. Serve immediately for the best flavor and texture.

NOTES

BOOST THE PROTEIN: Add grilled chicken, tofu, or tempeh to increase the protein content. Edamame or quinoa are also great additions for extra flavor and heartiness.

NUTRITIONAL ANALYSIS

PER SERVING: 330 calories; 24 g fat; 28 g carbohydrates; 8 g dietary fiber; 14 g sugars; 9 g protein

The Build Your Bowl System Profile

- NON-STARCHY VEGETABLES: Arugula, watercress, cauliflower, cucumber, onion
- FRUITS: Berries
- WHOLE FOOD FATS: Almonds, olive oil
- FLAVOR ENHANCERS: Herbs, dressing

Japanese Cucumber & Seaweed Salad with Tempeh

Inspired by traditional Japanese flavors, this refreshing salad combines crisp cucumbers, nutrient-rich seaweed, and protein-packed tempeh, making it detox-friendly and *high in fiber.*

YIELD: 4 servings • **PREP TIME:** 20 minutes plus 10 minutes to marinate • **COOK TIME:** 15 minutes • **TOTAL TIME:** 45 minutes

FOR THE MISO SESAME VINAIGRETTE:

⅓ cup (80 ml) rice vinegar
2 tablespoons (30 ml) low-sodium soy sauce or tamari
2 tablespoons (30 ml) toasted sesame oil
2 teaspoons miso paste
1 to 2 teaspoons pure maple syrup or coconut nectar
2 teaspoons grated fresh ginger
Salt, to taste

FOR THE BOWL:

1 block (8 ounces, or 225 g) tempeh, cut into bite-size cubes
¼ cup (6 g) dried wakame seaweed, soaked, drained, and chopped
2 large Japanese cucumbers, thinly sliced
1 medium carrot, shredded
3 small radishes, thinly sliced
Salt and pepper, to taste
1 ripe avocado, peeled, pitted, and sliced
1 tablespoon (9 g) toasted sesame seeds
1 scallion, thinly sliced

MAKE THE DRESSING: In a small bowl, whisk together all the dressing ingredients. Adjust the seasoning with salt to taste. The dressing doubles as a marinade for the tempeh.

PREPARE THE TEMPEH: Place the tempeh cubes in a shallow dish and pour half the dressing over them. Marinate for 10 to 30 minutes. Heat a non-stick pan over medium heat. Add the marinated tempeh and cook for 5 to 7 minutes on each side, or until browned and slightly crispy. Remove from the heat.

SOAK THE SEAWEED: In a small bowl, soak the seaweed in warm water for 5 to 10 minutes until softened. Drain, chop, and set aside.

BUILD THE BOWL: In a large bowl, combine the seaweed, cucumbers, carrot, and radishes. Toss with the remaining dressing until evenly coated. Adjust the seasoning with salt if necessary.

SERVE: Divide the salad evenly among four bowls. Top each with the tempeh, avocado, sesame seeds, and scallion. Serve immediately.

NOTES

CHOOSING SEAWEED: Wakame is a mild, nutrient-rich seaweed often found in dried form in the Asian food aisle, specialty stores, or online. If unavailable, you can use nori (sheets cut into strips) or arame, which are also common seaweeds with a slightly different texture.

MAKE IT HEARTIER: Serve with soba noodles, quinoa, or brown rice for added fiber and to make it more filling.

FLAVOR ENHANCERS: Add lime juice, red pepper flakes, or fresh herbs like cilantro or mint for extra flavor.

NUTRITIONAL ANALYSIS

PER SERVING: 305 calories; 22 g fat; 18 g carbohydrates; 4 g dietary fiber; 5 g sugars; 15 g protein

The Build Your Bowl System Profile

- NON-STARCHY VEGETABLES: Cucumbers, seaweed, carrot, radishes, scallions
- FRUITS: Avocado
- WHOLE FOOD FATS: Avocado, sesame seeds, sesame oil
- HIGH-QUALITY PROTEINS: Tempeh
- FLAVOR ENHANCERS: Dressing

Moroccan Carrot Bowl with Lentils

This Moroccan-inspired bowl blends antioxidant-packed spiced carrots, fiber-rich lentils, and fresh greens for a detoxifying boost.

YIELD: 4 servings • **PREP TIME:** 20 minutes • **COOK TIME:** 30 minutes • **TOTAL TIME:** 50 minutes

FOR THE LEMON GARLIC YOGURT DRESSING:

½ cup (120 g) plain Greek yogurt (whole milk or 2% reduced fat)
1 tablespoon (15 ml) fresh lemon juice
1 clove garlic, minced
Salt and pepper, to taste

FOR THE MOROCCAN-SPICED CARROTS:

4 large carrots, peeled and sliced into sticks
2 tablespoons (30 ml) extra-virgin olive oil
1 teaspoon ground cumin
1 teaspoon ground coriander
½ teaspoon ground cinnamon
¼ teaspoon ground turmeric
Salt and pepper, to taste

FOR THE BOWL:

1 cup (200 g) green or brown lentils
3 cups (720 ml) water or low-sodium vegetable broth
6 cups (180 g) baby spinach
½ red bell pepper, thinly sliced
½ cucumber, cubed
¼ cup (4 g) fresh cilantro, chopped
¼ cup (24 g) fresh mint, chopped
¼ cup (38 g) crumbled feta cheese (optional)

MAKE THE DRESSING: In a small bowl, whisk together the yogurt, lemon juice, garlic, salt, and pepper. Adjust the seasoning to taste.

PREPARE THE CARROTS: Preheat the oven to 400°F (200°C). Toss the carrots with the olive oil, cumin, coriander, cinnamon, turmeric, salt, and pepper. Spread evenly on a baking sheet and roast for 20 to 25 minutes, or until tender and slightly caramelized.

COOK THE LENTILS: Rinse the lentils under cold water. Add to a medium saucepan with the water. Bring to a boil over medium heat, then reduce the heat, cover, and simmer for 20 to 25 minutes, or until tender. Drain any excess liquid and set aside to cool.

BUILD THE BOWL: In a large bowl, combine the lentils, spinach, bell pepper, cucumber, cilantro, and mint. Drizzle with some of the dressing and toss gently to combine. Divide the mixture among four bowls, top with carrots, and drizzle with more dressing. Add crumbled feta, if using, and serve immediately.

NOTES

CLEANSING VARIATION: To make this bowl even more detox-friendly, cook the lentils in water instead of broth and skip the feta cheese. Adding extra fresh herbs and greens boosts its cleansing qualities, while the dressing keeps it bright and refreshing.

NUTRITIONAL ANALYSIS

PER SERVING: 350 calories; 12 g fat; 47 g carbohydrates; 9 g dietary fiber; 9 g sugars; 19 g protein

The Build Your Bowl System Profile

- **NON-STARCHY VEGETABLES:** Carrots, spinach, bell pepper, cucumber
- **WHOLE FOOD FATS:** Olive oil, cheese, yogurt
- **HIGH-QUALITY PROTEINS:** Cheese, yogurt
- **FIBER-RICH STARCHES:** Lentils
- **FLAVOR ENHANCERS:** Herbs, cheese, spices, dressing

Barley & Butter Lettuce Bowl

Blending the earthy richness of barley with colorful, crisp veggies, and a bright tarragon vinaigrette, this fiber-rich, antioxidant-packed bowl supports anti-inflammatory health while delivering a satisfying crunch and a burst of fresh, vibrant flavors.

YIELD: 4 servings • **PREP TIME:** 15 minutes • **COOK TIME:** 25 minutes • **TOTAL TIME:** 40 minutes

FOR THE TARRAGON VINAIGRETTE:

¼ cup (60 ml) extra-virgin olive oil
2 tablespoons (30 ml) apple cider vinegar
1 tablespoon (15 ml) fresh lemon juice
1 tablespoon (11 g) Dijon mustard
1 tablespoon (5 g) fresh tarragon, finely chopped
1 teaspoon pure honey or maple syrup (optional)
Salt and pepper, to taste

FOR THE BOWL:

1 cup (170 g) pearled barley
3 cups (720 ml) water or low-sodium vegetable broth
Salt
8 cups (440 g) bite-size butter lettuce pieces
1 cup (100 g) radishes, thinly sliced
1 cup (150 g) cherry tomatoes, halved
½ English cucumber, thinly sliced
½ medium red onion, thinly sliced
¼ cup (10 g) fresh tarragon, chopped
¼ cup (30 g) slivered almonds (optional)

MAKE THE DRESSING: In a small bowl, whisk together the olive oil, vinegar, lemon juice, mustard, tarragon, and honey (if using). Season with salt and pepper to taste.

COOK THE BARLEY: Rinse the barley under cold water. In a medium saucepan, combine the barley with the water and a pinch of salt. Bring to a boil, then reduce the heat to low. Cover and simmer for 25 minutes, or until the barley is tender and has absorbed most of the liquid. Drain any excess liquid, then set aside to cool.

BUILD THE BOWL: In a large serving bowl, layer the lettuce, barley, radishes, tomatoes, cucumber, and onion. Drizzle with the dressing and gently toss to combine. Divide the salad among four bowls, sprinkle each with fresh tarragon and almonds, if using. Serve immediately.

NOTES

ADD SOME PROTEIN: Add grilled chicken, shrimp, or tofu to make this bowl a more protein-rich and filling main course.

REDUCE THE CARBS: For a heartier texture with fewer carbohydrates, reduce the barley to ½ cup (85 g) uncooked, or substitute cauliflower rice or zucchini noodles.

NUTRITIONAL ANALYSIS

PER SERVING: 360 calories; 19 g fat; 41 g carbohydrates; 10 g dietary fiber; 6 g sugars; 9 g protein

The Build Your Bowl System Profile

- NON-STARCHY VEGETABLES: Lettuce, radishes, tomatoes, cucumber, onion
- WHOLE FOOD FATS: Olive oil, almonds
- FIBER-RICH STARCHES: Barley
- FLAVOR ENHANCERS: Tarragon, dressing

Broccoli & Quinoa Ginger Bowl

Packed with anti-inflammatory ingredients, this bowl provides a satisfying crunch from the fresh veggies, while the ginger sesame vinaigrette adds a tangy, nutty kick.

YIELD: 4 servings • **PREP TIME:** 15 minutes • **COOK TIME:** 15 minutes • **TOTAL TIME:** 30 minutes

FOR THE GINGER SESAME VINAIGRETTE:

¼ cup (60 ml) apple cider vinegar
2 tablespoons (30 ml) tamari or low-sodium soy sauce
1 tablespoon (8 g) grated fresh ginger
1 tablespoon (20 g) pure maple syrup or honey
2 tablespoons (30 ml) toasted sesame oil
1 clove garlic, minced
Salt and pepper to taste

FOR THE BOWL:

1 cup (170 g) quinoa (tricolored if available)
2 cups (480 ml) water or low-sodium vegetable broth
1 medium head broccoli, chopped into florets (3 to 4 cups, or 255 to 340 g)
1 large carrot, shredded
½ small red cabbage, thinly sliced
½ cup (78 g) shelled edamame, cooked
¼ cup (4 g) fresh cilantro, chopped
¼ cup (24 g) fresh mint, chopped
2 scallions, thinly sliced
¼ cup (35 g) toasted sesame seeds or sunflower seeds

MAKE THE DRESSING: Combine all the dressing ingredients in a small bowl, shaker, or mason jar. Whisk or shake until well mixed. Season with salt and pepper to taste.

COOK THE QUINOA: Rinse and drain the quinoa. Add to a medium saucepan with the water. Bring to a boil over medium heat, then reduce to a simmer. Cover and cook for 15 to 20 minutes, or until the quinoa has absorbed all the liquid. Fluff with a fork and set aside to cool.

PREPARE THE BROCCOLI: Bring a large pot of salted water to a boil. Fill a large mixing bowl halfway with ice and add cold water, leaving 2 to 3 inches (5 to 7 cm) of space at the top. Add the broccoli florets to the boiling water and blanch for 2 to 3 minutes until bright green and tender-crisp, then transfer to the ice bath. Alternatively, steam the broccoli for 3 to 4 minutes, covered, over 1 to 2 inches (2.5 to 5 cm) of boiling water on medium-high heat. After cooking, transfer to an ice bath, drain, and set aside.

BUILD THE BOWL: In a large bowl, combine the cooked quinoa, broccoli, carrot, cabbage, edamame, cilantro, mint, and scallions. Toss gently to mix the ingredients evenly. Drizzle the dressing over the salad and toss until well coated. Sprinkle with toasted sesame seeds before serving.

NOTES

THICKEN THE DRESSING: For a creamier texture, whisk in 1 to 2 tablespoons (15 to 30 g) of silken tofu or plain Greek yogurt with the dressing.

BOOST THE PROTEIN: Add grilled chicken, shrimp, or tofu to increase the protein content.

FLAVOR ENHANCERS: Add a squeeze of fresh lime juice, red pepper flakes for heat, or extra fresh herbs like cilantro or basil for more flavor.

NUTRITIONAL ANALYSIS

PER SERVING: 440 calories; 24 g fat; 45 g carbohydrates; 8 g dietary fiber; 9 g sugars; 12 g protein

The Build Your Bowl System Profile

- NON-STARCHY VEGETABLES: Broccoli, carrot, cabbage, herbs, scallions
- WHOLE FOOD FATS: Seeds, sesame oil
- HIGH-QUALITY PROTEINS: Quinoa, edamame
- FIBER-RICH STARCHES: Quinoa
- FLAVOR ENHANCERS: Herbs, dressing

Refreshing Green Bean & Almond Salad

This refreshing, no-fuss salad features crisp green beans, toasted almonds, and a vibrant mix of fresh vegetables, all tossed in a lemon garlic vinaigrette infused with turmeric for a detoxifying boost.

YIELD: 4 servings • **PREP TIME:** 15 minutes • **COOK TIME:** 10 minutes • **TOTAL TIME:** 25 minutes

FOR THE LEMON GARLIC VINAIGRETTE:

3 tablespoons (45 ml) extra-virgin olive oil
2 tablespoons (30 ml) fresh lemon juice
1 clove garlic, minced
1 teaspoon Dijon mustard
1 teaspoon pure honey or maple syrup (optional)
¼ teaspoon ground turmeric
½ teaspoon ground cumin
Salt and pepper, to taste

FOR THE BOWL:

1 pound (450 g) fresh green beans, trimmed
½ yellow bell pepper, thinly sliced
¼ small red onion, thinly sliced
½ cup (75 g) cherry tomatoes, halved
1 small carrot, peeled and julienned
½ cup (60 g) toasted almonds, sliced or chopped
2 tablespoons (10 g) fresh tarragon, chopped

MAKE THE DRESSING: In a small bowl, whisk together the olive oil, lemon juice, garlic, mustard, honey (if using), turmeric, cumin, salt, and pepper until well combined.

BLANCH THE GREEN BEANS: Bring a large pot of salted water to a boil. Fill a large mixing bowl halfway with ice and add cold water, leaving 2 to 3 inches (5 to 7 cm) of space at the top. Add the green beans to the boiling water and cook for 3 to 4 minutes until they are tender-crisp and bright green. Immediately transfer to the ice water to stop the cooking process. Drain and set aside.

BUILD THE BOWL: In a large bowl, combine the blanched green beans, bell pepper, onion, tomatoes, and carrot. Pour the dressing over the salad and toss gently to coat all the ingredients. Top with almonds and garnish with tarragon. Serve immediately.

NOTES

BOOST THE PROTEIN: For extra protein and a more filling salad, add a handful of cooked quinoa or steamed edamame.

FLAVOR ENHANCERS: Sprinkle with smoked paprika or red pepper flakes for a touch of heat. You can also swap tarragon for fresh basil or mint to change up the flavor profile.

NUTRITIONAL ANALYSIS

PER SERVING: 260 calories; 20 g fat; 19 g carbohydrates; 6 g dietary fiber; 7 g sugars; 7 g protein

The Build Your Bowl System Profile

- **NON-STARCHY VEGETABLES:** Green beans, yellow bell pepper, cherry tomatoes, red onion, carrot
- **WHOLE FOOD FATS:** Almonds, olive oil
- **HIGH-QUALITY PROTEINS:** Almonds
- **FLAVOR ENHANCERS:** Dressing, tarragon, turmeric, cumin

Turmeric Quinoa & Edamame Bowl

Chock-full of antioxidants and wholesome goodness, this bowl combines turmeric's anti-inflammatory benefits with the protein and fiber power of quinoa and edamame. Fresh veggies add crunch and color, while a zesty citrus dressing ties it all together.

YIELD: 4 servings • **PREP TIME:** 15 minutes • **COOK TIME:** 20 minutes • **TOTAL TIME:** 35 minutes

FOR THE CITRUS HERB VINAIGRETTE:

¼ cup (60 ml) fresh orange juice
2 tablespoons (30 ml) fresh lime juice
1 tablespoon (15 ml) extra-virgin olive oil
1 tablespoon (15 ml) white wine vinegar
1 teaspoon pure honey or maple syrup (optional)
1 tablespoon (1 g) fresh cilantro, finely chopped
1 clove garlic, minced
Salt and pepper, to taste

FOR THE BOWL:

1 cup (170 g) quinoa (red or black if available)
2 cups (480 ml) water or low-sodium vegetable broth
1 tablespoon (7 g) ground turmeric
1 cup (155 g) shelled edamame, cooked and cooled
1 red bell pepper, diced
1 medium carrot, shredded
½ cucumber, sliced into half-moons
2 scallions with tops and bulbs, thinly sliced
¼ cup (4 g) fresh cilantro, chopped
1 avocado, peeled, pitted, and diced
¼ cup (35 g) toasted sunflower seeds

MAKE THE DRESSING: In a small bowl, whisk together the orange juice, lime juice, olive oil, vinegar, honey (if using), cilantro, and garlic. Season with salt and pepper to taste.

COOK THE QUINOA: Rinse and drain the quinoa. In a medium saucepan, combine the quinoa, water, and turmeric. Bring to a boil over medium heat, then reduce to a simmer. Cover and cook for 15 to 20 minutes, or until the quinoa has absorbed all the liquid. Fluff with a fork and set aside to cool.

BUILD THE BOWL: In a large bowl, combine the quinoa, edamame, bell pepper, carrot, cucumber, scallions, and cilantro. Pour the dressing over the mixture and gently toss to combine. Divide the salad among four bowls, top with avocado and sunflower seeds, and serve immediately.

NOTES

ADD MORE PROTEIN: Boost the protein content by adding grilled salmon, tofu, or tempeh for a heartier, more satisfying meal.

FLAVOR ENHANCERS: Fresh herbs like mint, tarragon, or shiso can enhance the bowl's flavors even more. For a spicy kick, add a pinch of red pepper flakes or smoked paprika to the dressing.

NUTRITIONAL ANALYSIS

PER SERVING: 390 calories; 18 g fat; 49 g carbohydrates; 10 g dietary fiber; 9 g sugars; 13 g protein

The Build Your Bowl System Profile

- **NON-STARCHY VEGETABLES:** Bell pepper, carrot, cucumber, scallions
- **FRUITS:** Avocado
- **WHOLE FOOD FATS:** Avocado, sunflower seeds, olive oil
- **HIGH-QUALITY PROTEINS:** Quinoa, edamame
- **FIBER-RICH STARCHES:** Quinoa
- **FLAVOR ENHANCERS:** Turmeric, cilantro, dressing

Mixed Beetroot & Jicama Salad

Packed with anti-inflammatory and antioxidant-rich ingredients, this colorful bowl features the earthy sweetness of roasted beets, the crispness of jicama, and the creamy tang of goat cheese, all topped with a refreshing lemon honey vinaigrette.

YIELD: 4 servings • **PREP TIME:** 20 minutes • **COOK TIME:** 50 minutes • **TOTAL TIME:** 1 hour 10 minutes

FOR THE LEMON HONEY VINAIGRETTE:

2 tablespoons (30 ml) extra-virgin olive oil
2 tablespoons (30 ml) fresh lemon juice
1 tablespoon (15 ml) apple cider vinegar
4½ teaspoons (30 g) pure honey, or to taste
1 teaspoon Dijon mustard
1 clove garlic, minced
1 to 2 tablespoons (15 to 30 ml) water or low-sodium vegetable broth, as needed (optional)
Salt and pepper, to taste

FOR THE BOWL:

2 medium beets (ideally red and golden)
1 tablespoon (15 ml) extra-virgin olive oil
Salt and pepper, to taste
8 cups (480 g) chopped Swiss chard
1 Granny Smith apple, cored and diced
½ jicama, peeled and diced
¼ red onion, diced
½ cup (75 g) crumbled goat cheese
½ cup (75 g) pistachios, shelled and chopped
Chopped fresh mint or basil, for garnish (optional)

MAKE THE DRESSING: Add all the dressing ingredients to a small bowl, shaker, or mason jar. Whisk or shake until well mixed.

PREPARE THE BEETS: Rinse and scrub the beets thoroughly, then dry and trim the tops and bottoms. Cut them in half. Preheat the oven to 400°F (200°C). Place the beets in a lightly greased baking dish, drizzle with the olive oil, and season with salt and pepper. Cover the dish with foil and roast for 50 to 60 minutes, or until tender. Let the beets cool for 5 to 10 minutes before peeling (or leave the skins on). Slice into cubes and set aside.

BUILD THE BOWL: Lay out the Swiss chard in a large bowl and mix with half the dressing. Add the beets, apple, jicama, and onion, then toss with more dressing. Divide the salad among four bowls and top each with goat cheese and pistachios. Garnish with fresh mint or basil, if using. Serve immediately.

NOTES

CUSTOMIZE YOUR GREENS: Substitute Swiss chard with spinach, arugula, or beet greens if the beets come with tops.

FLEXIBLE SUBSTITUTIONS: Red and golden beets are typically available year-round, but if not, use all red beets. For a crunchy alternative to jicama, consider using water chestnuts or radishes.

ADD MORE PROTEIN: Enhance the salad with grilled shrimp, roasted turkey slices, or quinoa for a protein boost.

NUTRITIONAL ANALYSIS

PER SERVING: 335 calories; 21 g fat; 31 g carbohydrates; 10 g dietary fiber; 17 g sugars; 9 g protein

The Build Your Bowl System Profile

- NON-STARCHY VEGETABLES: Swiss chard, beets, jicama, onion
- FRUITS: Apple
- WHOLE FOOD FATS: Olive oil, pistachios, cheese
- HIGH-QUALITY PROTEINS: Cheese
- FLAVOR ENHANCERS: Herbs, dressing

Sweet Potato & Kale Crunch Bowl

With roasted sweet potatoes, crisp apple, and massaged kale drizzled in a creamy balsamic tahini dressing, this bowl is packed with antioxidant and anti-inflammatory ingredients that strike the perfect balance of savory, sweet, and tangy flavors.

YIELD: 4 servings • **PREP TIME:** 15 minutes • **COOK TIME:** 30 minutes • **TOTAL TIME:** 45 minutes

FOR THE BALSAMIC TAHINI DRESSING:

¼ cup (60 g) tahini
2 tablespoons (30 ml) balsamic vinegar
1 teaspoon pure maple syrup
1 clove garlic, minced
½ teaspoon grated fresh ginger
1 tablespoon (15 ml) extra-virgin olive oil
2 to 3 tablespoons (30 to 45 ml) water, as needed
Salt and pepper, to taste

FOR THE BOWL:

2 large sweet potatoes, peeled and diced
2 tablespoons (30 ml) extra-virgin olive oil
1 teaspoon smoked paprika
½ teaspoon ground turmeric
Salt and pepper, to taste
6 to 8 cups (400 to 535 g) chopped stemmed kale
1 medium cucumber, cubed
1 medium apple (Granny Smith or Fuji), diced
½ small red onion, diced
¼ cup (40 g) toasted pepitas
¼ cup (30 g) dried cranberries (optional)

MAKE THE DRESSING: In a small bowl, combine the tahini, vinegar, maple syrup, garlic, ginger, and olive oil. Whisk until well mixed, then gradually add the water, 1 tablespoon (15 ml) at a time, until you reach your desired consistency. Season with salt and pepper to taste. For a smoother texture, blend the dressing in a blender or food processor.

ROAST THE SWEET POTATOES: Preheat the oven to 400°F (200°C). Toss the diced sweet potatoes with olive oil, paprika, turmeric, salt, and pepper. Spread them evenly on a baking sheet and roast for 25 to 30 minutes, stirring halfway through, until tender and caramelized. Set aside to cool slightly.

BUILD THE BOWL: In a large bowl, combine the kale and a few tablespoons of dressing. Gently massage the kale for 1 to 2 minutes until it softens and turns bright green. Add the cucumber, apple, onion, and sweet potatoes to the massaged kale. Drizzle with more dressing and toss gently to combine, adjusting the amount of dressing to taste. Divide the salad evenly among four bowls. Top with pepitas and dried cranberries (if using). Serve immediately with any extra dressing on the side.

NOTES

ADD MORE PROTEIN: Layers like grilled chicken, lamb meatballs, and marinated tofu provide extra protein while still maintaining the salad's balance of flavors and textures.

FLAVOR ENHANCERS: Add a sprinkle of feta cheese, lemon zest, or fresh herbs like parsley or cilantro for a boost.

NUTRITIONAL ANALYSIS

PER SERVING: 375 calories; 23 g fat; 40 g carbohydrates; 7 g dietary fiber; 19 g sugars; 8 g protein

The Build Your Bowl System Profile

- **NON-STARCHY VEGETABLES:** Kale, cucumber, onion
- **FRUITS:** Apple, dried cranberries
- **WHOLE FOOD FATS:** Tahini, seeds, olive oil
- **FIBER-RICH STARCHES:** Sweet potatoes
- **FLAVOR ENHANCERS:** Dried cranberries, seasonings, dressing

Roasted Beet & Endive Salad

This nutrient-dense bowl features antioxidant-rich, anti-inflammatory ingredients like roasted beets, leafy greens, carrots, nuts, and olive oil. Finished with a savory balsamic vinaigrette, it's a flavorful, wellness-boosting meal.

YIELD: 4 servings • **PREP TIME:** 10 minutes • **COOK TIME:** 50 minutes • **TOTAL TIME:** 1 hour

FOR THE SAVORY BALSAMIC VINAIGRETTE:

¼ cup (60 ml) extra-virgin olive oil
2 tablespoons (30 ml) balsamic vinegar
1 tablespoon (11 g) Dijon mustard
1 tablespoon (20 g) pure honey or maple syrup
Salt and pepper, to taste

FOR THE BOWL:

3 medium beets with tops
1 to 2 tablespoons (15 to 30 ml) extra-virgin olive oil
Salt and pepper, to taste
2 large endive heads (white or red), thinly sliced
2 cups (40 g) baby arugula
2 medium carrots, shredded or ribboned
1 medium cucumber, thinly sliced
1 small red onion, thinly sliced
½ cup (60 g) toasted pecans or walnuts, chopped
½ cup (80 g) fresh pomegranate seeds

MAKE THE DRESSING: Add all the dressing ingredients to a small bowl, shaker, or mason jar. Whisk or shake until mixed well. Adjust the seasoning to taste.

PREPARE THE BEETS: Trim and set aside the beet greens (you will use these later). Rinse and scrub the beets thoroughly, then dry and trim off the tops and bottoms. Preheat the oven to 400°F (200°C). Cut the beets in half and place them in a lightly greased baking dish. Drizzle with olive oil, season with salt and pepper, and cover the dish with foil. Roast for 50 to 60 minutes, or until the beets are tender. Once done, let them cool for 5 to 10 minutes before peeling (or leave the skins on). Slice into cubes and set aside.

MIX THE GREENS: Wash, dry, and chop the reserved beet greens. In a large bowl, combine the greens with the endive and arugula. Lightly toss the greens with a small amount of the dressing to evenly coat them.

BUILD THE BOWL: Add the carrots, cucumber, onion, and beets to the bowl of mixed greens. Drizzle with more dressing and toss gently to combine. Divide the salad evenly among four bowls. Top each with a sprinkle of nuts and pomegranate seeds. Serve immediately to enjoy the freshest flavor and best texture.

NOTES

BOOST THE PROTEIN: Add grilled chicken, shrimp, salmon, or plant-based options like chickpeas or quinoa.

FLAVOR ENHANCERS: Crumbled goat cheese or feta, fresh herbs like parsley, and a squeeze of lemon bring extra brightness and flavor to the bowl.

NUTRITIONAL ANALYSIS

PER SERVING: 395 calories; 28 g fat; 34 g carbohydrates; 14 g dietary fiber; 17 g sugars; 8 g protein

The Build Your Bowl System Profile

- NON-STARCHY VEGETABLES: Beets, beet greens, endive, arugula, carrots, cucumber, onion
- WHOLE FOOD FATS: Nuts, olive oil
- FLAVOR ENHANCERS: Dressing

Citrus Herb Marinated–Mushroom Salad

Combining perfectly marinated mushrooms with layers of vibrant veggies, this nourishing bowl is a delicious way to support your body's natural cleansing and anti-inflammatory processes.

YIELD: 4 servings • **PREP TIME:** 20 minutes plus 30 minutes to marinate • **COOK TIME:** 0 minutes • **TOTAL TIME:** 50 minutes

FOR CITRUS HERB VINAIGRETTE:

¼ cup (60 ml) extra-virgin olive oil
3 tablespoons (45 ml) apple cider vinegar
2 tablespoons (30 ml) fresh lemon juice
1 tablespoon (11 g) Dijon mustard
1 clove garlic, minced
¼ teaspoon dried oregano
¼ teaspoon dried basil
1 teaspoon pure honey or maple syrup (optional)
Salt and pepper, to taste

FOR THE BOWL:

6 ounces (170 g) baby bella (or cremini) mushrooms, sliced or chopped
4 to 6 cups (80 to 100 g) arugula
1 small head broccoli, chopped into florets
1 large cucumber, cubed
1 large yellow bell pepper, diced
½ medium red onion, diced
2 medium carrots, shredded
1 cup (150 g) cherry tomatoes, halved
¼ cup (40 g) hemp seeds
2 tablespoons (8 g) fresh parsley, finely chopped (optional)

MAKE THE DRESSING: Add all the dressing ingredients to a small bowl, shaker, or mason jar. Whisk or shake until well combined. This dressing also doubles as a marinade for the mushrooms.

MARINATE THE MUSHROOMS: Place the mushrooms in a medium bowl and pour half the dressing over them. Toss to coat the mushrooms evenly, then cover and refrigerate for 30 minutes to 2 hours to let the flavors meld.

BUILD THE BOWL: In a large mixing bowl, combine the arugula, broccoli, cucumber, bell pepper, onion, carrots, and tomatoes. Add the marinated mushrooms and hemp seeds, then toss everything together until well coated. Drizzle with the remaining dressing and toss again if needed. Divide the salad among four bowls, garnish with fresh parsley if desired, and serve immediately as a refreshing main or side dish.

NOTES

MAKE IT YOUR OWN: Add fresh herbs like cilantro or dill for a flavorful twist. For extra protein, top the salad with grilled chicken, tofu, or tempeh.

NUTRITIONAL ANALYSIS

PER SERVING: 265 calories; 19 g fat; 20 g carbohydrates; 4 g dietary fiber; 8 g sugars; 8 g protein

The Build Your Bowl System Profile

- **NON-STARCHY VEGETABLES:** Mushrooms, arugula, broccoli, cucumber, bell pepper, onion, carrots, tomatoes
- **WHOLE FOOD FATS:** Hemp seeds, olive oil
- **HIGH-QUALITY PROTEINS:** Hemp seeds
- **FLAVOR ENHANCERS:** Parsley, dressing

Acknowledgments

I consider myself incredibly fortunate to have found a way to intertwine my passion, purpose, and pastime into the work I do today. But my journey didn't begin this way.

When I made the decision to leave my career as a research scientist in 2016 and pursue a path as a full-time healthy living coach and wellness expert, I didn't fully know what I was stepping into. Then, like so many others during the global pandemic of 2020, I completely lost my way. Clients disappeared, contracts dried up, and personal loss left me searching for direction. During this difficult time, I found comfort in creating eclectic salad bowls.

As fate would have it, my husband, Woody, gifted me a beautiful wooden salad bowl for Christmas that year. That simple gift sparked my transformation into "That Salad Lady" and laid the foundation for everything this brand has become.

Salad bowls, with their endless combinations of vibrant fruits, vegetables, and whole foods, hold a special significance for me—much like a treasured keepsake or long-awaited gift. Yet, standing at the crossroads of my life, I wondered, "Is this really what I'm going to do after over a decade in academia?"

I worried I might disappoint those who had supported me, but instead, I was met with unwavering encouragement. To all those who stood by me, I am forever grateful.

Woody, my husband, the technical genius, the gift-giver of that life-changing bowl, and my biggest fan—your belief in me has kept me going through it all.

My boys, Ramsey and Little Aubrey, my constant source of strength and motivation, thank you for inspiring me to keep building my bowl and my life.

To my mother, Gladys, and late father, Aubrey, who nurtured my creativity and encouraged me to embrace cooking and family life at a young age—your influence is woven into everything I do, in and out of the kitchen.

Nekohl, my big sister, thank you for being both a second mother and a best friend, always guiding and supporting my dreams from childhood to now.

I also want to thank my mentors, Toby, Helen, and Sandie, for guiding me through academia and continuing to support me through this new chapter.

Kim, my dear friend, thank you for being one of That Salad Lady's first supporters, always sharing your tomatoes and herbs when I needed them, taste-testing recipes and lending a helping hand.

To Hilary and the team at Fair Winds Press, thank you for believing in me and helping me bring this cookbook to life.

And to all the followers and supporters of That Salad Lady—your encouragement since day one has fueled every step of this journey. This cookbook wouldn't exist without your support, and for that, I'm truly grateful.

Finally, to you, the reader—whether you've been with me from the start or are just discovering That Salad Lady, thank you for letting me share my passion with you. I hope this cookbook brings as much joy to your kitchen as it has to mine.

About the Author

Dr. Nina Cherie Franklin, PhD, is a globally recognized wellness expert, healthy living coach, and the creator of the popular blog and brand "That Salad Lady." With a PhD in Kinesiology, Nutrition, and Rehabilitation along with numerous certifications in related fields, she brings over twenty-five years of experience in health, wellness, and fitness. Dr. Franklin has dedicated her career to empowering people to lead healthier lives through practical, sustainable lifestyle changes.

As a leading advocate for making healthy living more approachable and inclusive, Dr. Franklin has contributed to scientific journals and national media outlets, challenging industry norms with fresh, evidence-based perspectives on nutrition.

Her unique approach is deeply rooted in both academic expertise and personal experiences overcoming chronic anxiety, food addiction, and obesity.

As a wife and working mother, including to a child with special needs, she intimately understands the challenges of balancing wellness with a busy life and is passionate about helping others do the same.

Through "That Salad Lady," Dr. Franklin couples her scientific knowledge with a passion for salad making, teaching people how to build nourishing, flavorful bowls that support overall wellness. *The Build Your Bowl Salad Cookbook* is an extension of her mission to help people feel confident and in control of their eating habits, making healthy eating both accessible and enjoyable.

Whether contributing to scientific discussions or helping everyday people improve their relationship with food, Dr. Franklin continues to inspire positive lifestyle changes—one delicious salad at a time.

Index

T

V

W

Z